Memory Dump Analysis Anthology

Volume 8a

Dmitry Vostokov
Software Diagnostics Institute

OpenTask

Published by OpenTask, Republic of Ireland

OpenTask books are available through booksellers and distributors worldwide. For further information or comments send requests to press@opentask.com.

A CIP catalog record for this book is available from the British Library.

ISBN-13: 978-1-908043-53-5 (Paperback)

First printing, 2014

Revision 2.0 (July 2015)

Table of Contents

Preface 7

About the Author 9

PART 1: Professional Crash Dump Analysis and Debugging 11

    Software Diagnostics Professional Certification 11
    Three Roads to Kernel Space 13

PART 2: Crash Dump Analysis Patterns 15

    Design Value 15
    Hidden IRP 16
    Tampered Dump 17
    Wait Chain (RTL_RESOURCE) 29
    Memory Fluctuation (Process Heap) 35
    Last Object 37
    Rough Stack Trace 39
    Past Stack Trace 43
    Stack Trace (I/O Request) 46
    Stack Trace (File System Filters) 48
    Stack Trace (Database) 51
    Wait Chain (Modules) 56
    Insufficient Memory (Stack Trace Database) 57
    Insufficient Memory (Region) 63
    Memory Leak (Regions) 65
    Invalid Handle (Managed Space) 69
    Ghost Thread 77
    Dry Weight 79
    Exception Module 80

PART 3: Memory Forensics 83

    Memory Forensics Professional Certification 83
    Native Memory Forensics 84

PART 4: A Bit of Science and Philosophy 85

Memory Symmetry Breaking 85
Memoevolutionism.. 86
Entropy as Memory and Memory as Entropy..................................... 87
Notes on Memoidealism 88
Welcome to Memorianism 89
United Memory Lands, Memorianites, EthnOS 90
Quotes from Memoriarch 91
Pattern-Oriented Philosophy 92

PART 5: Software Trace Analysis Patterns 93

Hidden Facts 93
Back Trace 95
Blackout 97
Missing Message 99
Use Case Trail 101
Event Sequence Phase 103
Milestones 105
File Size 107
Singleton Event 108
Visitor Trace 110

PART 6: Fun with Crash Dumps 111

Debugging Slang and Proverbs 111

PUS.. 111
Coollect 111
Dump-out.. 111
LOGIC 111
DiagNose... 112
Consolidation 112
No Pass a Run! 112
ID IoT Zone 112
Putty in Someone's Hands.. 112
DisPatched vs. DESPatched.. 112
Programmatica Nervosa 113

GOTCHA *113*
Pan-o-RAM-ic *113*
VLSI *113*
Debugging Proverb *113*

Space Opera 114
If Programmers Were Writers 115
My Computer Celebrates Halloween 116
Look, there's a Bug! 117
Diagnostics in Science Fiction 118
Hard Copy Natives 119

PART 7: Software Narratology **121**

Malnarratives 121
Higher-Order Pattern Narratives (Analyzing Diagnostic Analysis) ... 123

PART 8: Software Diagnostics, Troubleshooting, and Debugging ... **127**

A Pattern Language for Performance Analysis 127
The Timeless Way of Diagnostics 128
Pattern-Oriented Debugging Process 130

PART 9: Art and Visualization **133**

Café WoW 133
Bang Debugging 134
Bug Hunter 135
Glass of Water Dump 136
Memory Dump Analysis 137
Organic Incidents and Bad Stench 138

PART 10: Miscellaneous **139**

Book Discovery 139
Quotes 140

Appendix **143**

6

Crash Dump Analysis Checklist 143

Index of WinDbg Commands 147

Notes.. 149

Preface

This reference volume consists of revised, edited, cross-referenced and thematically organized articles from Software Diagnostics Institute (DumpAnalysis.org + TraceAnalysis.org) and Software Diagnostics Library (former Crash Dump Analysis blog, DumpAnalysis.org/blog). Most of the selected articles are about software diagnostics, debugging, crash dump analysis, software trace and log analysis, malware analysis, and memory forensics. They were written in June 2014 - November 2014. We hope this reference is useful for:

- Software engineers developing and maintaining products on Windows platforms;
- Technical support and escalation engineers dealing with complex software issues;
- Quality assurance engineers testing software on Windows platforms;
- Security researchers, reverse engineers, malware and memory forensics analysts;
- Software trace and log analysis articles are of interest to users of any platform.

If you encounter any error, please contact me using this form:

http://www.dumpanalysis.org/contact

or send me a personal message using this contact e-mail:

dmitry.vostokov@dumpanalysis.org

Alternatively, via Twitter @DumpAnalysis

Facebook page and group:

http://www.facebook.com/DumpAnalysis

http://www.facebook.com/TraceAnalysis

http://www.facebook.com/groups/dumpanalysis

[This page is intentionally left blank]

About the Author

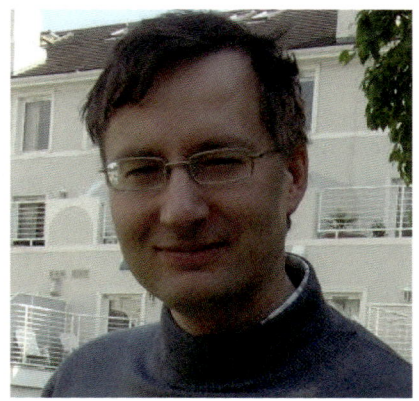

Dmitry Vostokov is an internationally recognized expert, speaker, educator, scientist and author. He is the founder of pattern-oriented software diagnostics, forensics and prognostics discipline and Software Diagnostics Institute (DA+TA: DumpAnalysis.org + TraceAnalysis.org). Vostokov has also authored more than 30 books on software diagnostics, forensics and problem-solving, memory dump analysis, debugging, software trace and log analysis, reverse engineering, and malware analysis. He has more than 20 years of experience in software architecture, design, development and maintenance in a variety of industries including leadership, technical and people management roles. Dmitry also founded OpenTask Iterative and Incremental Publishing (OpenTask.com), Software Diagnostics Services (former Memory Dump Analysis Services) PatternDiagnostics.com and Software Prognostics. In his spare time, he presents various topics on Debugging.TV and explores Software Narratology, an applied science of software stories that he pioneered.

[This page is intentionally left blank]

PART 1: Professional Crash Dump Analysis and Debugging

Software Diagnostics Professional Certification

Software Diagnostics Services[1] offers a certification in pattern-oriented software diagnostics for software technical support and escalation engineers, software engineers, and quality assurance engineers with the following assessment areas:

- pattern-oriented memory dump analysis
- pattern-oriented software trace and log analysis

The focus is on unintentional software behavior such related to crashes, resource consumption (CPU, memory leaks) and hangs. For intentional software behavior, there is Memory Forensics Professional certification (page 83) under development. The Windows track tests the ability to recognize patterns using the following analysis tools: WinDbg from Microsoft Debugging Tools for Windows and Process Monitor.

The certification has the following features:

- Two-factor certification:

  - The first phase is based on real software execution artifacts, not on questions;
  - The second phase involves questions about analysis results to assess understanding;
  - Each certificate has its own verifiable CID (Certificate ID).

- Each assessment score transcript has its unique PID.TID (Performance ID and Transcript ID).
- Each candidate gets a set of unique memory dumps and software traces.
- Evaluation of individual and overall exam group performance (when there is a sufficient number of candidates and may be postponed initially until the right group size).

---

[1] http://www.patterndiagnostics.com/Certified-Software-Diagnostics-Professional

- Second free attempt after one month if the applicant does not pass an assessment.

Three Roads to Kernel Space

Here we newly update our original "The Road to Kernel Space" article (Volume1, page 664). The previous update was called "Moving to Kernel Space (with an eye on security)" and published in October 2010 in Software Diagnostics Library[2].

Since then, many new books mentioning kernel space and Windows device drivers were published. We realized that not only one road but three of them were available based on your needs. Of course, there are intersections. Common to all roads is Windows Internals book set (6th version at the time of this writing).

If you take device driver writer road, you need these books:

- The Windows 2000 Device Driver Book: A Guide for Programmers, 2nd edition
- Windows NT Device Driver Development
- Developing Windows NT Device Drivers: A Programmer's Handbook
- Programming the Microsoft Windows Driver Model, 2nd edition
- Developing Drivers with the Windows Driver Foundation

If you take reversing, memory forensics, and malware analysis road you need these books:

- Rootkits: Subverting the Windows Kernel
- The Rootkit Arsenal: Escape and Evasion in the Dark Corners of the System, 2nd edition
- Practical Reverse Engineering: X86, X64, Arm, Windows Kernel, Reversing Tools, and Obfuscation
- The Art of Memory Forensics: Detecting Malware and Threats in Windows, Linux, and Mac Memory
- Practical Malware Analysis: The Hands-On Guide to Dissecting Malicious Software

---

[2]   http://www.dumpanalysis.org/blog/index.php/2010/10/30/moving-to-kernel-space-updated-references-with-an-eye-on-security/

- Malware Analyst's Cookbook and DVD: Tools and Techniques for Fighting Malicious Code
- Accelerated Windows Malware Analysis with Memory Dumps: Training Course Transcript and WinDbg Practice Exercises[3]

If you take software support crash and hang memory dump analysis road you need these books:

- Accelerated Windows Memory Dump Analysis: Training Course Transcript and WinDbg Practice Exercises with Notes, Third Edition[4]
- Advanced Windows Memory Dump Analysis with Data Structures: Training Course Transcript and WinDbg Practice Exercises with Notes, Second Edition[5]

Also, there are few optional books for any road such as:

- Windows NT File System Internals
- Windows NT/2000 Native API Reference

---

[3] http://www.dumpanalysis.org/accelerated-windows-malware-analysis-book

[4] http://www.dumpanalysis.org/accelerated-windows-memory-dump-analysis-book

[5] http://www.dumpanalysis.org/advanced-windows-memory-dump-analysis-book

PART 2: Crash Dump Analysis Patterns

Design Value

The pattern called **Small Value** (Volume 7, page 191) deals with easily recognizable values such as handles, timeouts, mouse pointer coordinates, enumeration values, and window messages. There is another kind of values, for example, 256 (+/- 1) or some other round value. Here we can also add some regular patterns in hex representation such as window handles or flags, for example, 0×10008000. Such designed values may fall into some module range, the so-called **Coincidental Symbolic Information** (Volume 1, page 390) pattern. They may not necessarily be stack trace parameters (which can also be **False Function Parameters**, Volume 2, page 173). If we see a design value in the output of WinDbg commands, especially related to abnormal behavior patterns, then it might point to some reached design limitations. For example, **Blocked ALPC Queue** (Volume 6, page 34) may have a limitation on I/O completion port (Volume 1, page 653). We observed that when we had **ALPC Wait Chains** (Volume 3, page 97) in one unresponsive system:

```
0: kd> !alpc /p <port_address>
[...]
512 thread(s) are registered with port IO completion object:
[...]
```

Hidden IRP

Sometimes we suspect a particular thread doing I/O but IRP is missing in the output of **!thread** WinDbg command. Here the best way is to examine the list of IRPs and associated threads from the output of **!irpfind** command. Here is a synthesized example from a few **Virtualized** (Volume 4, page 131) Young System (Volume 2, page 335) crash dumps:

```
0: kd> !thread fffffa8004e2d280


THREAD fffffa8004e2d280 Cid 0004.0020 Teb: 0000000000000000
Win32Thread: 0000000000000000 WAIT: (Executive) KernelMode Non-
Alertable
fffff880009ec440 NotificationEvent
Not impersonating
[...]


0: kd> !irpfind


Irp [ Thread ] irpStack: (Mj,Mn) DevObj [Driver] MDL Process
[...]
fffffa800424e4e0 [fffffa8004e2d280] irpStack: (3, 0) fffffa8004ed6d40
[ \Driver\DriverA]
[...]
```

Now we can inspect the found IRP (**!irp** command) and device object (for example, by using **!devobj** and **!devstack** commands). Sometimes we can see the same IRP address as **Execution Residue** (Volume 2, page 239) among *"Args to Child"* values in the output of **!thread** command or **kv** (if the thread is current).

Tampered Dump

The availability of direct dump modification raises the possibility of such memory dumps specifically modified to alter structural and behavioral diagnostic patterns. For example, to suppress certain module involvement or introduce fictitious past objects and interaction traces such as **Execution Residue** (Volume 2, page 239) and **Module Hints** (Volume 6, page 92). There can be 2 types of such artifacts: *strong tampering* with new or altered information completely integrated into memory fabric and *weak tampering* to confuse inexperienced software support engineers and memory forensics analysts.

For example, in one such experimental process memory dump we see **Exception Stack Trace** (Volume 4, page 337) pointing to a problem in *calc* module:

```
0:003> k
Child-SP RetAddr Call Site
00000000`0244e858 000007fe`fd061430 ntdll!NtWaitForMultipleObjects+0xa
00000000`0244e860 00000000`76ec1723 KERNELBASE!WaitForMultipleObjectsEx+0xe8
00000000`0244e960 00000000`76f3b5e5
kernel32!WaitForMultipleObjectsExImplementation+0xb3
00000000`0244e9f0 00000000`76f3b767 kernel32!WerpReportFaultInternal+0x215
00000000`0244ea90 00000000`76f3b7bf kernel32!WerpReportFault+0x77
00000000`0244eac0 00000000`76f3b9dc kernel32!BasepReportFault+0x1f
00000000`0244eaf0 00000000`77153398 kernel32!UnhandledExceptionFilter+0x1fc
00000000`0244ebd0 00000000`770d85c8 ntdll! ?? ::FNODOBFM::`string'+0x2365
00000000`0244ec00 00000000`770e9d2d ntdll!_C_specific_handler+0x8c
00000000`0244ec70 00000000`770d91cf ntdll!RtlpExecuteHandlerForException+0xd
00000000`0244eca0 00000000`77111248 ntdll!RtlDispatchException+0x45a
00000000`0244f380 00000000`ffdbdb27 ntdll!KiUserExceptionDispatch+0x2e
00000000`0244fab0 00000000`76eb59ed calc!CTimedCalc::WatchDogThread+0xb2
00000000`0244faf0 00000000`770ec541 kernel32!BaseThreadInitThunk+0xd
00000000`0244fb20 00000000`00000000 ntdll!RtlUserThreadStart+0x1d
```

The default analysis command (**!analyze -v**) diagnoses "*stack corruption*":

```
FAULTING_IP:
kernel32!UnhandledExceptionFilter+1fc
00000000`76f3b9dc 448bf0 mov r14d,eax


EXCEPTION_RECORD: ffffffffffffffff -- (.exr 0xffffffffffffffff)
ExceptionAddress: 0000000076f3b9dc
(kernel32!UnhandledExceptionFilter+0x00000000000001fc)
ExceptionCode: 0244e9f0
ExceptionFlags: 00000000
NumberParameters: 0
```

<pre>
DEFAULT_BUCKET_ID: STACK_CORRUPTION

PRIMARY_PROBLEM_CLASS: STACK_CORRUPTION

BUGCHECK_STR: APPLICATION_FAULT_STACK_CORRUPTION

IP_ON_HEAP: 8d483674c33bfffa
The fault address in not in any loaded module, please check your
build's rebase log at
<releasedir>\bin\build_logs\timebuild\ntrebase.log for module which
may contain the address if it were loaded.

UNALIGNED_STACK_POINTER: 0000000076f3b767

STACK_TEXT:
00000000`00000000 00000000`00000000
calc!CTimedCalc::WatchDogThread+0x0

FOLLOWUP_IP:
calc!CTimedCalc::WatchDogThread+0
00000000`ffd92254 48895c2408 mov qword ptr [rsp+8],rbx
</pre>

Stored Exception (Volume 6, page 119) resembles signs of **Local Buffer Overflow** (Volume 1, page 461): segment register values and CPU flags have suspiciously invalid values, possibly from **Lateral Damage** (Volume 1, page 264):

<pre>
0:003> .ecxr
rax=0000000000000000 rbx=0000000000000001 rcx=000000000244ec30
rdx=000000000244ec30 rsi=0100000000000080 rdi=0000000000000158
rip=0000000076f3b9dc rsp=0000000076f3b767 rbp=0000000000000000
r8=0000000000000000 r9=ffffffffffffffff r10=0000000076f3b7bf
r11=000000000244ec30 r12=0000000000000001 r13=0000000000000000
r14=0000000000000000 r15=0000000000000000
iopl=0 nv up di pl nz na pe nc
cs=0000 ss=0000 ds=0266 es=0000 fs=0000 gs=0154 efl=00000000
kernel32!UnhandledExceptionFilter+0x1fc:
00000000`76f3b9dc 448bf0 mov r14d,eax

0:003> k
*** Stack trace for last set context - .thread/.cxr resets it
Child-SP RetAddr Call Site
00000000`76f3b767 8d483674`c33bfffa
kernel32!UnhandledExceptionFilter+0x1fc
00000000`76f3b847 5aa3e800`05bfac0d 0x8d483674`c33bfffa
00000000`76f3b84f ebffcf83`48ccfff9 0x5aa3e800`05bfac0d
00000000`76f3b857 8348c000`0409ba27 0xebffcf83`48ccfff9
00000000`76f3b85f 54dfe8cf`8b48ffcf 0x8348c000`0409ba27
00000000`76f3b867 4c02778d`db33fff9 0x54dfe8cf`8b48ffcf
</pre>

```
00000000`76f3b86f  4c000000`e024a48b  0x4c02778d`db33fff9
00000000`76f3b877  ffcf8348`04ebeb8b  0x4c000000`e024a48b
00000000`76f3b87f  fffc59e9`e8cc8b49  0xffcf8348`04ebeb8b
00000000`76f3b887  42e9c78b`0775c73b  0xfffc59e9`e8cc8b49
00000000`76f3b88f  fffa6fa9`e8000003  0x42e9c78b`0775c73b
00000000`76f3b897  32e9c033`0774c33b  0xfffa6fa9`e8000003
00000000`76f3b89f  fa7f3d8d`4c000003  0x32e9c033`0774c33b
00000000`76f3b8a7  de15ffcf`8b490006  0xfa7f3d8d`4c000003
00000000`76f3b8af  f9370d8b`4800000e  0xde15ffcf`8b490006
00000000`76f3b8b7  000014a1`15ff0006  0xf9370d8b`4800000e
00000000`76f3b8bf  840fc33b`48f08b4c  0x000014a1`15ff0006
00000000`76f3b8c7  f6158b48`00000099  0x840fc33b`48f08b4c
00000000`76f3b8cf  0238c281`480006f3  0xf6158b48`00000099
00000000`76f3b8d7  48cfe8c8`8b480000  0x0238c281`480006f3
00000000`76f3b8df  8b4c7f74`c33bfff9  0x48cfe8c8`8b480000
00000000`76f3b8e7  888b4900`06f3dc05  0x8b4c7f74`c33bfff9
00000000`76f3b8ef  75083949`00000238  0x888b4900`06f3dc05
00000000`76f3b8f7  00000240`808b496c  0x75083949`00000238
00000000`76f3b8ff  8b415f75`08403949  0x00000240`808b496c
00000000`76f3b907  00024880`3b411040  0x8b415f75`08403949
00000000`76f3b90f  01040000`a9527500  0x00024880`3b411040
00000000`76f3b917  00025090`8d491874  0x01040000`a9527500
00000000`76f3b91f  c68a4418`488d4900  0x00025090`8d491874
00000000`76f3b927  c33a0000`117315ff  0xc68a4418`488d4900
00000000`76f3b92f  4e15ffcf`8b493374  0xc33a0000`117315ff
00000000`76f3b937  ff41cc8b`4900000e  0x4e15ffcf`8b493374
00000000`76f3b93f  00028c84`0fc63bd6  0xff41cc8b`4900000e
00000000`76f3b947  00028484`0fc73b00  0x00028c84`0fc63bd6
00000000`76f3b94f  6ee7e819`75c33b00  0x00028484`0fc73b00
00000000`76f3b957  c0331074`c33bfffa  0x6ee7e819`75c33b00
00000000`76f3b95f  cf8b4900`000270e9  0xc0331074`c33bfffa
00000000`76f3b967  8b490000`0e1b15ff  0xcf8b4900`000270e9
00000000`76f3b96f  3b000013`e215ffcc  0x8b490000`0e1b15ff
00000000`76f3b977  0253e9c7`8b0775c7  0x3b000013`e215ffcc
00000000`76f3b97f  41fff959`4ae80000  0x0253e9c7`8b0775c7
00000000`76f3b987  c6844100`000002be  0x41fff959`4ae80000
00000000`76f3b98f  15ff0000`023d850f  0xc6844100`000002be
00000000`76f3b997  850f20a8`00000f65  0x15ff0000`023d850f
00000000`76f3b99f  245c8948`0000022f  0x850f20a8`00000f65
00000000`76f3b9a7  448d4c3e`4e8d4520  0x245c8948`0000022f
00000000`76f3b9af  ffc933d6`8b416024  0x448d4c3e`4e8d4520
00000000`76f3b9b7  7cc33b00`0009f415  0xffc933d6`8b416024
00000000`76f3b9bf  730a7024`64ba0f0f  0x7cc33b00`0009f415
00000000`76f3b9c7  00000205`e9c68b07  0x730a7024`64ba0f0f
00000000`76f3b9cf  cc8b49d6`8bfb8b44  0x00000205`e9c68b07
00000000`76f3b9d7  f08b44ff`fffdc4e8  0xcc8b49d6`8bfb8b44
00000000`76f3b9df  e9c03307`7508f883  0xf08b44ff`fffdc4e8
00000000`76f3b9e7  7506f883`000001e9  0xe9c03307`7508f883
00000000`76f3b9ef  c33bfffa`6e4be810  0x7506f883`000001e9
00000000`76f3b9f7  0001d4e9`c0330774  0xc33bfffa`6e4be810
00000000`76f3b9ff  86850f04`fe834100  0x0001d4e9`c0330774
00000000`76f3ba07  0000024a`ba000001  0x86850f04`fe834100
```

```
00000000`76f3ba0f 00b841ce`8b45c933 0x0000024a`ba000001
00000000`76f3ba17 fff7a249`e8000010 0x00b841ce`8b45c933
00000000`76f3ba1f 0775c33b`48e88b4c 0xfff7a249`e8000010
00000000`76f3ba27 48000001`a6e9c033 0x0775c33b`48e88b4c
00000000`76f3ba2f 24448948`3024448d 0x48000001`a6e9c033
00000000`76f3ba37 0000f024`8c8d4c20 0x24448948`3024448d
00000000`76f3ba3f 49000001`25b84100 0x0000f024`8c8d4c20
00000000`76f3ba47 8a0fe8cf`8b48d58b 0x49000001`25b84100
00000000`76f3ba4f 4166097c`c33bfffe 0x8a0fe8cf`8b48d58b
00000000`76f3ba57 39fe450f`44005d39 0x4166097c`c33bfffe
00000000`76f3ba5f 850f0000`00f0249c 0x39fe450f`44005d39
00000000`76f3ba67 240c8b49`000000bc 0x850f0000`00f0249c
00000000`76f3ba6f 40244489`48016348 0x240c8b49`000000bc
00000000`76f3ba77 24448948`10418b48 0x40244489`48016348
00000000`76f3ba7f 75c00000`06398148 0x24448948`10418b48
00000000`76f3ba87 480b7203`18798318 0x75c00000`06398148
00000000`76f3ba8f 50244489`4830418b 0x480b7203`18798318
00000000`76f3ba97 eb50245c`89481ceb 0x50244489`4830418b
00000000`76f3ba9f 8b480b72`18713915 0xeb50245c`89481ceb
00000000`76f3baa7 eb502444`89482041 0x8b480b72`18713915
00000000`76f3baaf 02ba5024`5c894805 0xeb502444`89482041
00000000`76f3bab7 0b721851`39000000 0x02ba5024`5c894805
00000000`76f3babf 24448948`28418b48 0x0b721851`39000000
00000000`76f3bac7 58245c89`4805eb58 0x24448948`28418b48
00000000`76f3bacf ba1d3808`74fb3b44 0x58245c89`4805eb58
00000000`76f3bad7 48d68b02`740006fd 0xba1d3808`74fb3b44
00000000`76f3badf 48000000`e824848d 0x48d68b02`740006fd
00000000`76f3bae7 20245489`28244489 0x48000000`e824848d
00000000`76f3baef c0334540`244c8d4c 0x20245489`28244489
00000000`76f3baf7 000144b9`04508d41 0xc0334540`244c8d4c
00000000`76f3baff ba00000d`7215ffd0 0x000144b9`04508d41
00000000`76f3bb07 8c8bc223`c0000000 0xba00000d`7215ffd0
00000000`76f3bb0f b8c23b00`0000e824 0x8c8bc223`c0000000
00000000`76f3bb17 89c8440f`00000006 0xb8c23b00`0000e824
00000000`76f3bb1f 07eb0000`00e8248c 0x89c8440f`00000006
00000000`76f3bb27 44000000`e8248c8b 0x07eb0000`00e8248c
00000000`76f3bb2f 7403f983`5d74fb3b 0x44000000`e8248c8b
00000000`76f3bb37 000000f0`249c3909 0x7403f983`5d74fb3b
00000000`76f3bb3f 0006fd4d`058a4f74 0x000000f0`249c3909
00000000`76f3bb47 f85f5ce8`4b75c33a 0x0006fd4d`058a4f74
00000000`76f3bb4f 448b3b75`5c5838ff 0xf85f5ce8`4b75c33a
00000000`76f3bb57 894c2824`44893024 0x448b3b75`5c5838ff
00000000`76f3bb5f 08244c8b`4d20246c 0x894c2824`44893024
00000000`76f3bb67 fec2c748`24048b4d 0x08244c8b`4d20246c
00000000`76f3bb6f b6e8cf8b`48ffffff 0xfec2c748`24048b4d
00000000`76f3bb77 fd130db6`0fffffea 0xb6e8cf8b`48ffffff
00000000`76f3bb7f 88ce4c0f`c33b0006 0xfd130db6`0fffffea
00000000`76f3bb87 ebfb8b00`06fd080d 0x88ce4c0f`c33b0006
00000000`76f3bb8f 3a0006fc`fe058a29 0xebfb8b00`06fd080d
00000000`76f3bb97 8b240c8b`491874c3 0x3a0006fc`fe058a29
00000000`76f3bb9f 060f15ff`cf8b4811 0x8b240c8b`491874c3
00000000`76f3bba7 0000f824`bc8b0000 0x060f15ff`cf8b4811
```

```
00000000`76f3bbaf  00f824bc`8b07eb00  0x0000f824`bc8b0000
00000000`76f3bbb7  331074eb`3b4c0000  0x00f824bc`8b07eb00
00000000`76f3bbbf  49000080`00b841d2  0x331074eb`3b4c0000
00000000`76f3bbc7  8bfff74b`5ae8cd8b  0x49000080`00b841d2
00000000`76f3bbcf  c48148c6`8b02ebc7  0x8bfff74b`5ae8cd8b
00000000`76f3bbd7  5e415f41`000000a0  0xc48148c6`8b02ebc7
00000000`76f3bbdf  c35b5e5f`5c415d41  0x5e415f41`000000a0
00000000`76f3bbe7  158ead00`00000090  0xc35b5e5f`5c415d41
00000000`76f3bbef  00000200`00000053  0x158ead00`00000090
00000000`76f3bbf7  09bc2400`00002500  0x00000200`00000053
00000000`76f3bbff  00000000`09b42400  0x09bc2400`00002500
00000000`76f3bc07  7e023553`158ead00  0x9b42400
00000000`76f3bc0f  00000400`00000a19  0x7e023553`158ead00
00000000`76f3bc17  09b42000`09bc2000  0x00000400`00000a19
00000000`76f3bc1f  445352bb`03197e00  0x09b42000`09bc2000
00000000`76f3bc27  4c886225`48e28953  0x445352bb`03197e00
00000000`76f3bc2f  4fb29af4`dfbb8344  0x4c886225`48e28953
00000000`76f3bc37  72656b00`0000020e  0x4fb29af4`dfbb8344
00000000`76f3bc3f  64702e32`336c656e  0x72656b00`0000020e
00000000`76f3bc47  00000000`00000062  0x64702e32`336c656e
```

We check for any **Hidden Exceptions** (Volume 1, page 271) and find it was **NULL Data Pointer** (Volume 3, page 131):

```
0:003> .cxr
Resetting default scope


0:003> k
Child-SP RetAddr Call Site
00000000`0244e858 000007fe`fd061430 ntdll!NtWaitForMultipleObjects+0xa
00000000`0244e860 00000000`76ec1723 KERNELBASE!WaitForMultipleObjectsEx+0xe8
00000000`0244e960 00000000`76f3b5e5
kernel32!WaitForMultipleObjectsExImplementation+0xb3
00000000`0244e9f0 00000000`76f3b767 kernel32!WerpReportFaultInternal+0x215
00000000`0244ea90 00000000`76f3b7bf kernel32!WerpReportFault+0x77
00000000`0244eac0 00000000`76f3b9dc kernel32!BasepReportFault+0x1f
00000000`0244eaf0 00000000`77153398 kernel32!UnhandledExceptionFilter+0x1fc
00000000`0244ebd0 00000000`770d85c8 ntdll! ?? ::FNODOBFM::`string'+0x2365
00000000`0244ec00 00000000`770e9d2d ntdll!_C_specific_handler+0x8c
00000000`0244ec70 00000000`770d91cf ntdll!RtlpExecuteHandlerForException+0xd
00000000`0244eca0 00000000`77111248 ntdll!RtlDispatchException+0×45a
00000000`0244f380 00000000`ffdbdb27 ntdll!KiUserExceptionDispatch+0×2e
00000000`0244fab0 00000000`76eb59ed calc!CTimedCalc::WatchDogThread+0xb2
00000000`0244faf0 00000000`770ec541 kernel32!BaseThreadInitThunk+0xd
00000000`0244fb20 00000000`00000000 ntdll!RtlUserThreadStart+0×1d


0:003> dps 00000000`0244eca0 00000000`0244fab0
00000000`0244eca0 00000000`02450000
00000000`0244eca8 00000000`76fadda0 kernel32!__PchSym_ <PERF> (kernel32+0x10dda0)
00000000`0244ecb0 00000000`00012f00
00000000`0244ecb8 00000000`7711920a ntdll!RtlDosApplyFileIsolationRedirection_Ustr+0x3da
00000000`0244ecc0 00000000`00000005
00000000`0244ecc8 00000000`00000000
00000000`0244ecd0 00000000`00000000
00000000`0244ecd8 00000000`00000000
```

```
00000000`0244ece0 00000000`0244fb20
00000000`0244ece8 00000000`00000000
00000000`0244ecf0 00000000`77202dd0 ntdll!CsrPortMemoryRemoteDelta <PERF> (ntdll+0x142dd0)
00000000`0244ecf8 00000000`00000000
00000000`0244ed00 00000000`00000000
00000000`0244ed08 00000000`02450000
00000000`0244ed10 00000000`771e8180 ntdll!`string'+0xc040
00000000`0244ed18 00000000`0244b000
00000000`0244ed20 00000000`0244f250
00000000`0244ed28 00000000`770c0000 ntdll!RtlDeactivateActivationContext <PERF> (ntdll+0x0)
00000000`0244ed30 00000000`770ec541 ntdll!RtlUserThreadStart+0x1d
00000000`0244ed38 00000000`770c0000 ntdll!RtlDeactivateActivationContext <PERF> (ntdll+0x0)
00000000`0244ed40 00000000`77202dd0 ntdll!CsrPortMemoryRemoteDelta <PERF> (ntdll+0x142dd0)
00000000`0244ed48 00000000`0244fb20
00000000`0244ed50 00000000`771d7718 ntdll!LdrpDefaultExtension
00000000`0244ed58 00000000`0244ed80
00000000`0244ed60 00000000`770d852c ntdll!_C_specific_handler
00000000`0244ed68 00000000`771e8180 ntdll!`string'+0xc040
00000000`0244ed70 00000000`0244f250
00000000`0244ed78 00000000`00000000
00000000`0244ed80 00000000`00000000
00000000`0244ed88 00000000`00000000
00000000`0244ed90 00000000`00000000
00000000`0244ed98 00000000`00000000
00000000`0244eda0 00000000`00000000
00000000`0244eda8 00000000`00000000
00000000`0244edb0 00001f80`00000000
00000000`0244edb8 00000000`00000033
00000000`0244edc0 00010246`002b0000
00000000`0244edc8 00000000`00000000
00000000`0244edd0 00000000`00000000
00000000`0244edd8 00000000`00000000
00000000`0244ede0 00000000`00000000
00000000`0244ede8 000007fe`ff3625c0 msctf!s_szCompClassName
00000000`0244edf0 00000000`00200000
00000000`0244edf8 00000000`0244ee40
00000000`0244ee00 00000000`0244ee40
00000000`0244ee08 00000000`0244ee40
00000000`0244ee10 00000000`00000000
00000000`0244ee18 00000000`0244fb70
00000000`0244ee20 00000000`00000000
00000000`0244ee28 00000000`00000000
00000000`0244ee30 00000000`00000000
00000000`0244ee38 000007fe`fd602790 ole32!`string'
00000000`0244ee40 00000000`00292170
00000000`0244ee48 00000000`770e7a33 ntdll!LdrpFindOrMapDll+0x138
00000000`0244ee50 00000000`0244ef68
00000000`0244ee58 00000000`00000000
00000000`0244ee60 00000000`00000000
00000000`0244ee68 00000000`00000000
00000000`0244ee70 00000000`00000000
00000000`0244ee78 00000000`00000000
00000000`0244ee80 00000000`0000027f
00000000`0244ee88 00000000`00000000
00000000`0244ee90 00000000`00000000
00000000`0244ee98 0000ffff`00001f80
00000000`0244eea0 00000000`00000000
00000000`0244eea8 00000000`00000000
00000000`0244eeb0 00000000`00000000
00000000`0244eeb8 00000000`00000000
00000000`0244eec0 00000000`00000000
00000000`0244eec8 00000000`00000000
00000000`0244eed0 00000000`00000000
00000000`0244eed8 00000000`00000000
00000000`0244eee0 00000000`00000000
00000000`0244eee8 00000000`00000000
00000000`0244eef0 00000000`00000000
00000000`0244eef8 00000000`00000000
00000000`0244ef00 00000000`00000000
00000000`0244ef08 00000000`00000000
```

```
00000000`0244ef10  00000000`00000000
00000000`0244ef18  00000000`00000000
00000000`0244ef20  00000000`00000000
00000000`0244ef28  00000000`771192a8 ntdll!LdrpApplyFileNameRedirection+0x2d3
00000000`0244ef30  00000000`00000000
00000000`0244ef38  00000000`00000000
00000000`0244ef40  00000000`00000000
00000000`0244ef48  00000000`02080000
00000000`0244ef50  00000000`0244f028
00000000`0244ef58  00000000`0244f020
00000000`0244ef60  00000000`00000000
00000000`0244ef68  00000000`00000000
00000000`0244ef70  00000000`00000000
00000000`0244ef78  000007fe`fd602848 ole32!`string'
00000000`0244ef80  00000000`00000000
00000000`0244ef88  00000000`00000000
00000000`0244ef90  00000000`00000000
00000000`0244ef98  00000000`00000000
00000000`0244efa0  00000000`00000000
00000000`0244efa8  00000000`00000000
00000000`0244efb0  00000000`00000000
00000000`0244efb8  00000000`00000000
00000000`0244efc0  00000000`00000000
00000000`0244efc8  00000000`00000000
00000000`0244efd0  00000000`00000000
00000000`0244efd8  00000000`00000000
00000000`0244efe0  00000000`00000000
00000000`0244efe8  00000000`00000000
00000000`0244eff0  00000000`00000000
00000000`0244eff8  00000000`00000000
00000000`0244f000  00000000`00000000
00000000`0244f008  00000000`00000000
00000000`0244f010  00000000`00000000
00000000`0244f018  00000000`00000000
00000000`0244f020  00000000`0244f038
00000000`0244f028  00000000`0000011b
00000000`0244f030  00000000`024d0000
00000000`0244f038  00000080`001a024d
00000000`0244f040  00000000`01c0c8a0
00000000`0244f048  00000000`002f0101
00000000`0244f050  00000000`00000000
00000000`0244f058  00000000`00000022
00000000`0244f060  00000000`002f9b00
00000000`0244f068  00000000`01bd5390
00000000`0244f070  00000000`002f7c00
00000000`0244f078  00000000`01bd5580
00000000`0244f080  00000000`01bd57b0
00000000`0244f088  00000000`002f9b00
00000000`0244f090  00000000`00000000
00000000`0244f098  00000024`00000003
00000000`0244f0a0  00000000`002e91b0
00000000`0244f0a8  00000000`00000022
00000000`0244f0b0  00000000`771d5430 ntdll!RtlpInterceptorRoutines
00000000`0244f0b8  00000000`00000000
00000000`0244f0c0  00000000`00000010
00000000`0244f0c8  00000000`01bd0000
00000000`0244f0d0  00000000`00000008
00000000`0244f0d8  00000000`00000001
00000000`0244f0e0  00000000`01bd0288
00000000`0244f0e8  00000000`77113448 ntdll!RtlAllocateHeap+0xe4
00000000`0244f0f0  00000000`00000000
00000000`0244f0f8  00000000`00000001
00000000`0244f100  000002b2`000f002f
00000000`0244f108  00000000`01bd5780
00000000`0244f110  00000000`00250230
00000000`0244f118  00000000`000000df
00000000`0244f120  00000000`002551a0
00000000`0244f128  00000000`00255210
00000000`0244f130  00000000`002f9b00
00000000`0244f138  00000000`002551a0
```

```
00000000`0244f140 00000000`000000df
00000000`0244f148 00000000`10000010
00000000`0244f150 00000000`00250230
00000000`0244f158 00000000`00000000
00000000`0244f160 00000000`00250498
00000000`0244f168 00000000`0025026c
00000000`0244f170 00000000`002f9b00
00000000`0244f178 00000000`002551a0
00000000`0244f180 00000000`00000022
00000000`0244f188 00000000`76fd88b8 user32!GetPropW+0x4d
00000000`0244f190 00000000`00002974
00000000`0244f198 00000000`76fd88b8 user32!GetPropW+0x4d
00000000`0244f1a0 00000000`00250230
00000000`0244f1a8 00000000`76fd7931 user32!IsWindow+0x9
00000000`0244f1b0 00000000`002ed6d0
00000000`0244f1b8 00000000`76fd7931 user32!IsWindow+0x9
00000000`0244f1c0 00000000`00000000
00000000`0244f1c8 00000000`01c0c8d0
00000000`0244f1d0 00000000`01c0c8a0
00000000`0244f1d8 00000000`00000000
00000000`0244f1e0 00000000`00000008
00000000`0244f1e8 00000000`01bd0000
00000000`0244f1f0 00000000`00000000
00000000`0244f1f8 00000000`770f41c8 ntdll!RtlpReAllocateHeap+0x178
00000000`0244f200 00000000`00000002
00000000`0244f208 00000000`00000002
00000000`0244f210 00000000`00000000
00000000`0244f218 000007fe`4f00024d
00000000`0244f220 00000000`00000000
00000000`0244f228 000007fe`fb601381 uxtheme!CThemeWnd::_PreDefWindowProc+0x31
00000000`0244f230 00000000`00000082
00000000`0244f238 00000000`00000000
00000000`0244f240 00000000`7a337100
00000000`0244f248 00000000`01c0c8c0
00000000`0244f250 00000000`00000003
00000000`0244f258 00000000`76eb59e0 kernel32!BaseThreadInitThunk
00000000`0244f260 00000000`ffdbdb32 calc!CTimedCalc::Start+0xa9
00000000`0244f268 00000000`ffd90000 calc!CCalculatorController::CCalculatorController <PERF>
(calc+0x0)
00000000`0244f270 00000000`ffe0ac64 calc!_dyn_tls_init_callback <PERF> (calc+0x7ac64)
00000000`0244f278 00000000`76ea0000 kernel32!TestResourceDataMatchEntry <PERF>
(kernel32+0x0)
00000000`0244f280 00000000`76fadda0 kernel32!__PchSym_ <PERF> (kernel32+0x10dda0)
00000000`0244f288 00000000`770c0000 ntdll!RtlDeactivateActivationContext <PERF> (ntdll+0x0)
00000000`0244f290 00000000`77202dd0 ntdll!CsrPortMemoryRemoteDelta <PERF> (ntdll+0x142dd0)
00000000`0244f298 00000000`76fd760e user32!RealDefWindowProcW+0x5a
00000000`0244f2a0 00000000`00000001
00000000`0244f2a8 000007fe`fb600037 uxtheme!operator delete <PERF> (uxtheme+0x37)
00000000`0244f2b0 00000000`01bd0158
00000000`0244f2b8 00000000`00000082
00000000`0244f2c0 00000000`00000000
00000000`0244f2c8 00000000`00000003
00000000`0244f2d0 00000000`000111f2
00000000`0244f2d8 00000000`00000054
00000000`0244f2e0 00000000`00000000
00000000`0244f2e8 00000000`00000000
00000000`0244f2f0 00000000`00000001
00000000`0244f2f8 00000000`01c11c60
00000000`0244f300 00000000`0244f462
00000000`0244f308 00000000`01bd0230
00000000`0244f310 00000000`00000000
00000000`0244f318 00000000`00000000
00000000`0244f320 00000000`00000000
00000000`0244f328 00000000`14010015
00000000`0244f330 00000000`01c11570
00000000`0244f338 00000000`00000000
00000000`0244f340 00000000`00000000
00000000`0244f348 00000000`00000000
00000000`0244f350 00000000`00009c40
00000000`0244f358 00000000`00000000
```

```
00000000`0244f360  00000000`00000000
00000000`0244f368  00000000`00000000
00000000`0244f370  00000000`00002710
00000000`0244f378  00000000`77111248  ntdll!KiUserExceptionDispatch+0x2e
00000000`0244f380  00000000`0244f870
00000000`0244f388  00000000`0244f380
00000000`0244f390  00000000`00000000
00000000`0244f398  00000000`00000000
00000000`0244f3a0  000007fe`fb63fb40  uxtheme!$$VProc_ImageExportDirectory
00000000`0244f3a8  00000000`00000ad5
00000000`0244f3b0  00001f80`0010005f
00000000`0244f3b8  0053002b`002b0033
00000000`0244f3c0  00010246`002b002b
00000000`0244f3c8  00000000`00000000
00000000`0244f3d0  00000000`00000000
00000000`0244f3d8  00000000`00000000
00000000`0244f3e0  00000000`00000000
00000000`0244f3e8  00000000`00000000
00000000`0244f3f0  00000000`00000000
00000000`0244f3f8  00000000`0012c770
00000000`0244f400  00000000`00000000
00000000`0244f408  00000000`00000000
00000000`0244f410  00000000`00002710
00000000`0244f418  00000000`0244fab0
00000000`0244f420  00000000`00000000
00000000`0244f428  00000000`00000000
00000000`0244f430  00000000`00000000
00000000`0244f438  00000000`0244f938
00000000`0244f440  00000000`00962210
00000000`0244f448  00000000`00000000
00000000`0244f450  00000000`0244f9a0
00000000`0244f458  00000000`00009c40
00000000`0244f460  00000000`00000000
00000000`0244f468  00000000`00000000
00000000`0244f470  00000000`00000000
00000000`0244f478  00000000`ffdbdb27  calc!CTimedCalc::WatchDogThread+0xb2
00000000`0244f480  00000000`0000027f
00000000`0244f488  00000000`00000000
00000000`0244f490  00000000`00000000
00000000`0244f498  0000ffff`00001f80
00000000`0244f4a0  00000000`00000000
00000000`0244f4a8  00000000`00000000
00000000`0244f4b0  00000000`00000000
00000000`0244f4b8  00000000`00000000
00000000`0244f4c0  00000000`00000000
00000000`0244f4c8  00000000`00000000
00000000`0244f4d0  00000000`00000000
00000000`0244f4d8  00000000`00000000
00000000`0244f4e0  00000000`00000000
00000000`0244f4e8  00000000`00000000
00000000`0244f4f0  00000000`00000000
00000000`0244f4f8  00000000`00000000
00000000`0244f500  00000000`00000000
00000000`0244f508  00000000`00000000
00000000`0244f510  00000000`00000000
00000000`0244f518  00000000`00000000
00000000`0244f520  00000000`00000000
00000000`0244f528  00000000`00000000
00000000`0244f530  00000000`00000000
00000000`0244f538  00000000`00000000
00000000`0244f540  00000000`00000000
00000000`0244f548  00000000`00000000
00000000`0244f550  00000000`00000000
00000000`0244f558  00000000`00000000
00000000`0244f560  00000000`00000000
00000000`0244f568  00000000`00000000
00000000`0244f570  00000000`00000000
00000000`0244f578  00000000`00000000
00000000`0244f580  00000000`00000000
00000000`0244f588  00000000`00000000
```

```
00000000`0244f590 00000000`00000000
00000000`0244f598 00000000`00000000
00000000`0244f5a0 00000000`00000000
00000000`0244f5a8 00000000`00000000
00000000`0244f5b0 00000000`00000000
00000000`0244f5b8 00000000`00000000
00000000`0244f5c0 00000000`00000000
00000000`0244f5c8 00000000`00000000
00000000`0244f5d0 00000000`00000000
00000000`0244f5d8 00000000`00000000
00000000`0244f5e0 00000000`00000000
00000000`0244f5e8 00000000`00000000
00000000`0244f5f0 00000000`00000000
00000000`0244f5f8 00000000`00000000
00000000`0244f600 00000000`00000000
00000000`0244f608 00000000`00000000
00000000`0244f610 00000000`00000000
00000000`0244f618 00000000`00000000
00000000`0244f620 00000000`00000000
00000000`0244f628 00000000`00000000
00000000`0244f630 00000000`00000000
00000000`0244f638 00000000`00000000
00000000`0244f640 00000000`00000000
00000000`0244f648 00000000`00000000
00000000`0244f650 00000000`00000000
00000000`0244f658 00000000`00000000
00000000`0244f660 00000000`00000000
00000000`0244f668 fffff800`032d5e53
00000000`0244f670 00000000`00000002
00000000`0244f678 00000000`00000000
00000000`0244f680 00000000`01c11580
00000000`0244f688 00000000`00000082
00000000`0244f690 00000000`00000082
00000000`0244f698 00000000`000111e4
00000000`0244f6a0 00000000`00000002
00000000`0244f6a8 00000000`0244f6f0
00000000`0244f6b0 00000000`00000002
00000000`0244f6b8 00000000`00000000
00000000`0244f6c0 00000000`000111e4
00000000`0244f6c8 00000000`00000000
00000000`0244f6d0 00000000`00000082
00000000`0244f6d8 00000000`00000000
00000000`0244f6e0 00000000`00000000
00000000`0244f6e8 00000000`76fe76c2 user32!DefDlgProcW+0×36
00000000`0244f6f0 00000000`00000000
00000000`0244f6f8 00000000`00000000
00000000`0244f700 00000000`000111e4
00000000`0244f708 00000000`00000000
00000000`0244f710 00000000`00000082
00000000`0244f718 00000000`00000000
00000000`0244f720 00000000`0244f908
00000000`0244f728 00000000`76fd9bef user32!UserCallWinProcCheckWow+0×1cb
00000000`0244f730 00000000`00962210
00000000`0244f738 00000000`00000001
00000000`0244f740 00000000`00000000
00000000`0244f748 00000000`00000000
00000000`0244f750 00000000`0244f768
00000000`0244f758 00000000`0244f778
00000000`0244f760 00000000`00000001
00000000`0244f768 00000000`00000000
00000000`0244f770 00000000`00000000
00000000`0244f778 00000000`00000000
00000000`0244f780 00000000`00000048
00000000`0244f788 00000000`00000001
00000000`0244f790 00000000`00000000
00000000`0244f798 00000000`00000000
00000000`0244f7a0 00000000`00000070
00000000`0244f7a8 ffffffff`ffffffff
00000000`0244f7b0 ffffffff`ffffffff
00000000`0244f7b8 00000000`76fd9b43 user32!UserCallWinProcCheckWow+0×99
```

```
00000000`0244f7c0  00000000`76fd9bef  user32!UserCallWinProcCheckWow+0×1cb
00000000`0244f7c8  00000000`00000000
00000000`0244f7d0  00000000`00000000
00000000`0244f7d8  00000000`00000000
00000000`0244f7e0  00000000`00000000
00000000`0244f7e8  00000000`76fd72cb  user32!DispatchClientMessage+0xc3
00000000`0244f7f0  00000000`00000000
00000000`0244f7f8  00000000`770e46b4  ntdll!NtdllDialogWndProc_W
00000000`0244f800  00000000`00000000
00000000`0244f808  00000000`00000000
00000000`0244f810  00000000`00000000
00000000`0244f818  00000000`00000000
00000000`0244f820  00000000`00962238
00000000`0244f828  00000000`00000001
00000000`0244f830  00000000`00000000
00000000`0244f838  00000000`00000000
00000000`0244f840  00000000`00000000
00000000`0244f848  00000000`00000000
00000000`0244f850  00000730`fffffb30
00000000`0244f858  000004d0`fffffb30
00000000`0244f860  00000170`000000f0
00000000`0244f868  0000002c`00000001
00000000`0244f870  00000000`c0000005
00000000`0244f878  00000000`00000000
00000000`0244f880  00000000`ffdbdb27  calc!CTimedCalc::WatchDogThread+0xb2
00000000`0244f888  00000000`00000002
00000000`0244f890  00000000`00000000
00000000`0244f898  00000000`00000000
00000000`0244f8a0  00000000`00000000
00000000`0244f8a8  00000000`00000000
00000000`0244f8b0  00000000`00000000
00000000`0244f8b8  00000000`00000000
00000000`0244f8c0  00000000`00000000
00000000`0244f8c8  00000000`00000000
00000000`0244f8d0  00000000`00000000
00000000`0244f8d8  00000000`00000000
00000000`0244f8e0  00000000`00000000
00000000`0244f8e8  00000000`00000000
00000000`0244f8f0  00000000`00000000
00000000`0244f8f8  00000000`00000000
00000000`0244f900  00000000`00000000
00000000`0244f908  00000000`00962210
00000000`0244f910  00000000`ffdbdb27  calc!CTimedCalc::WatchDogThread+0xb2
00000000`0244f918  00000000`00000000
00000000`0244f920  00000000`00000000
00000000`0244f928  00000000`0244fab0
00000000`0244f930  00000000`77101530  ntdll!NtdllDispatchMessage_W
00000000`0244f938  00000000`76fe505b  user32!DialogBox2+0×2ec
00000000`0244f940  00000000`00000000
00000000`0244f948  00000000`00000000
00000000`0244f950  00000000`00000000
00000000`0244f958  00000000`00000000
00000000`0244f960  00000000`00000000
00000000`0244f968  00000000`00000000
00000000`0244f970  00000000`00000000
00000000`0244f978  00000000`00000000
00000000`0244f980  00000000`00000002
00000000`0244f988  00000000`000111f0
00000000`0244f990  00000271`0f689359
00000000`0244f998  00000000`00000030
00000000`0244f9a0  00000000`00000000
00000000`0244f9a8  00000000`00000000
00000000`0244f9b0  00000000`ffd90000  calc!CCalculatorController::CCalculatorController <PERF>
(calc+0×0)
00000000`0244f9b8  00000000`001a17e0
00000000`0244f9c0  00000000`00000000
00000000`0244f9c8  00000000`76fe4edd  user32!InternalDialogBox+0×135
00000000`0244f9d0  00000000`00000000
00000000`0244f9d8  00000000`ffdcedb0  calc!CTimedCalc::TimeOutDlgProc
00000000`0244f9e0  00000000`00000000
```

```
00000000`0244f9e8 00000000`00000000
00000000`0244f9f0 00000000`ffdcedb0 calc!CTimedCalc::TimeOutDlgProc
00000000`0244f9f8 00000000`00000000
00000000`0244fa00 00000000`00000001
00000000`0244fa08 00000000`00000000
00000000`0244fa10 00000000`00000000
00000000`0244fa18 00000000`00009c40
00000000`0244fa20 00000000`ffd90000 calc!CCalculatorController::CCalculatorController <PERF>
(calc+0×0)
00000000`0244fa28 00000000`76fe4f52 user32!DialogBoxIndirectParamAorW+0×58
00000000`0244fa30 00000000`001a17e0
00000000`0244fa38 00000000`00000000
00000000`0244fa40 00000000`ffdcedb0 calc!CTimedCalc::TimeOutDlgProc
00000000`0244fa48 00000000`ffdcedb0 calc!CTimedCalc::TimeOutDlgProc
00000000`0244fa50 00000000`00000000
00000000`0244fa58 00000000`00000001
00000000`0244fa60 00000000`ffd90000 calc!CCalculatorController::CCalculatorController <PERF>
(calc+0×0)
00000000`0244fa68 00000000`76fdd476 user32!DialogBoxParamW+0×66
00000000`0244fa70 ffffffff`ffffffff
00000000`0244fa78 00000000`00000000
00000000`0244fa80 00000000`ffdcedb0 calc!CTimedCalc::TimeOutDlgProc
00000000`0244fa88 00000000`00000000
00000000`0244fa90 00000000`00000000
00000000`0244fa98 00000000`00000000
00000000`0244faa0 00000000`00000000
00000000`0244faa8 00000000`ffdbdafa calc!CTimedCalc::WatchDogThread+0×72
00000000`0244fab0 00000000`00002710
```

Segment registers and flags look normal now:

```
0:003> .cxr 00000000`0244f380
rax=000000000012c770 rbx=0000000000002710 rcx=0000000000000000
rdx=0000000000000000 rsi=0000000000000000 rdi=0000000000000000
rip=00000000ffdbdb27 rsp=000000000244fab0 rbp=0000000000000000
r8=000000000244f938 r9=0000000000962210 r10=0000000000000000
r11=000000000244f9a0 r12=0000000000009c40 r13=0000000000000000
r14=0000000000000000 r15=0000000000000000
iopl=0   nv up ei pl zr na po nc
cs=0033 ss=002b ds=002b es=002b fs=0053 gs=002b efl=00010246
calc!CTimedCalc::WatchDogThread+0xb2:
00000000`ffdbdb27 488b01 mov rax,qword ptr [rcx]
ds:00000000`00000000=????????????????


0:003> k
*** Stack trace for last set context - .thread/.cxr resets it
Child-SP RetAddr Call Site
00000000`0244fab0 00000000`76eb59ed
calc!CTimedCalc::WatchDogThread+0xb2
00000000`0244faf0 00000000`770ec541 kernel32!BaseThreadInitThunk+0xd
00000000`0244fb20 00000000`00000000 ntdll!RtlUserThreadStart+0x1d
```

Wait Chain (RTL_RESOURCE)

Here we provide another variant of a general **Wait Chain** pattern (Volume 1, page 482) related to *RtlAcquireResourceShared* and *RtlAcquireResourceExclusive* calls:

```
THREAD fffffa8052d66060  Cid 03c0.3240  Teb: 000007fffff90000 Win32Thread:
0000000000000000 WAIT: (UserRequest) UserMode Non-Alertable
fffffa804a79ad50  Semaphore Limit 0x7fffffff
Impersonation token:  fffff8a01b19d060 (Level Impersonation)
DeviceMap                 fffff8a0035276c0
Owning Process            fffffa804a16b260      Image:         lsm.exe
Attached Process          N/A             Image:         N/A
Wait Start TickCount      73343513        Ticks: 1460259 (0:06:20:16.546)
Context Switch Count      17              IdealProcessor: 1
UserTime                  00:00:00.000
KernelTime                00:00:00.000
Win32 Start Address ntdll!TppWorkerThread (0x000000007735fbf0)
Stack Init fffff8800e870db0 Current fffff8800e870900
Base fffff8800e871000 Limit fffff8800e86b000 Call 0
Priority 9 BasePriority 8 UnusualBoost 0 ForegroundBoost 0 IoPriority 2
PagePriority 5
Kernel stack not resident.
Child-SP          RetAddr           Call Site
fffff880`0e870940 fffff800`01c76972 nt!KiSwapContext+0x7a
fffff880`0e870a80 fffff800`01c87d8f nt!KiCommitThreadWait+0x1d2
fffff880`0e870b10 fffff800`01f7b2be nt!KeWaitForSingleObject+0x19f
fffff880`0e870bb0 fffff800`01c801d3 nt!NtWaitForSingleObject+0xde
fffff880`0e870c20 00000000`773912fa nt!KiSystemServiceCopyEnd+0x13 (TrapFrame @
fffff880`0e870c20)
00000000`022ae6c8 00000000`773470b4 ntdll!NtWaitForSingleObject+0xa
00000000`022ae6d0 00000000`ff4013a3 ntdll!RtlAcquireResourceShared+0xd0
00000000`022ae710 00000000`ff401675 lsm!CAutoSharedLock::CAutoSharedLock+0x61
00000000`022ae7e0 00000000`ff402c68 lsm!CTSSession::getTerminal+0x21
00000000`022ae820 000007fe`fd8bff85 lsm!RpcGetEnumResult+0x202
00000000`022ae980 000007fe`fd8b4de2 RPCRT4!Invoke+0x65
00000000`022ae9e0 000007fe`fd8b17bd RPCRT4!NdrStubCall2+0x32a
00000000`022af000 000007fe`fd8b3254 RPCRT4!NdrServerCall2+0x1d
00000000`022af030 000007fe`fd8b33b6 RPCRT4!DispatchToStubInCNoAvrf+0x14
00000000`022af060 000007fe`fd8b3aa9 RPCRT4!RPC_INTERFACE::DispatchToStubWorker+0x146
00000000`022af180 000007fe`fd8b375d RPCRT4!LRPC_SCALL::DispatchRequest+0x149
00000000`022af260 000007fe`fd8d09ff RPCRT4!LRPC_SCALL::HandleRequest+0x20d
00000000`022af390 000007fe`fd8d05b5 RPCRT4!LRPC_ADDRESS::ProcessIO+0x3bf
00000000`022af4d0 00000000`7735b6bb RPCRT4!LrpcIoComplete+0xa5
00000000`022af560 00000000`7735ff2f ntdll!TppAlpcpExecuteCallback+0x26b
00000000`022af5f0 00000000`7713652d ntdll!TppWorkerThread+0x3f8
00000000`022af8f0 00000000`7736c541 kernel32!BaseThreadInitThunk+0xd
00000000`022af920 00000000`00000000 ntdll!RtlUserThreadStart+0x1d
```

These functions are undocumented, but ReactOS source code shows they all take a pointer to *RTL_RESOURCE* structure[6] that has handles to a shared and exclusive semaphores:

```
RTL_CRITICAL_SECTION    Lock
HANDLE                  SharedSemaphore
ULONG                   SharedWaiters
HANDLE                  ExclusiveSemaphore
ULONG                   ExclusiveWaiters
LONG                    NumberActive
HANDLE                  OwningThread
ULONG                   TimeoutBoost
PVOID                   DebugInfo
```

To double check that we disassemble *RtlAcquireResourceShared* and check the return address from *NtWaitForSingleObject* call (00000000`773470b4):

```
0: kd> .thread /r /p fffffa8052d66060
Implicit thread is now fffffa80`52d66060
Implicit process is now fffffa80`4a16b260
Loading User Symbols
.........................................

0: kd> uf ntdll!RtlAcquireResourceShared
[...]
ntdll!RtlAcquireResourceShared+0xc2:
00000000`773470a6 488b4b28    mov rcx,qword ptr [rbx+28h]
00000000`773470aa 4c8bc6      mov r8,rsi
00000000`773470ad 33d2        xor edx,edx
00000000`773470af e83ca20400  call ntdll!NtWaitForSingleObject
(00000000`773912f0)
00000000`773470b4 3d02010000  cmp eax,102h
00000000`773470b9 0f8402800600 je ntdll! ??
::FNODOBFM::`string'+0x12629 (00000000`773af0c1)
[...]
ntdll!RtlAcquireResourceShared:
00000000`77352af0 48895c2420  mov qword ptr [rsp+20h],rbx
00000000`77352af5 57          push rdi
00000000`77352af6 4883ec30    sub rsp,30h
00000000`77352afa 448b4944    mov r9d,dword ptr [rcx+44h]
00000000`77352afe 0fb6fa      movzx edi,dl
00000000`77352b01 488bd9      mov rbx,rcx
00000000`77352b04 4585c9      test r9d,r9d
00000000`77352b07 0f88a7000000 js ntdll!RtlAcquireResourceShared+0x65
```

---

[6] http://doxygen.reactos.org/da/d93/structRTL__RESOURCE.html

```
(00000000`77352bb4)
[...]
```

We see the handle is taken from [RBX+28], and we see that RBX was saved at the function prolog, and then the value of RCX was assigned to RBX. RCX as the first calling convention parameter should be a pointer to *RTL_RESOURCE* that has *RTL_CRITICAL_SECTION* as the first member, and its size is 0×28:

```
0: kd> dt ntdll!_RTL_CRITICAL_SECTION
ntdll!_RTL_CRITICAL_SECTION
+0x000 DebugInfo         : Ptr64 _RTL_CRITICAL_SECTION_DEBUG
+0x008 LockCount         : Int4B
+0x00c RecursionCount    : Int4B
+0x010 OwningThread      : Ptr64 Void
+0x018 LockSemaphore     : Ptr64 Void
+0x020 SpinCount         : Uint8B
```

Therefore [RBX+28] contains *SharedSemaphore* field that is assigned to RCX as a first parameter to *NtWaitForSingleObject*. The similar fragment of *RtlAcquireResourceExclusive* has [RBX+38] which 0×10 further than 0×28 and corresponds to *ExclusiveSemaphore* handle field:

```
ntdll!RtlAcquireResourceExclusive+0xd2:
00000000`770c2a12 488b4b38        mov     rcx,qword ptr [rbx+38h]
00000000`770c2a16 4c8bc6          mov     r8,rsi
00000000`770c2a19 33d2            xor     edx,edx
00000000`770c2a1b e8d0e80400      call    ntdll!NtWaitForSingleObject
(00000000`771112f0)
00000000`770c2a20 3d02010000      cmp     eax,102h
00000000`770c2a25 0f8401c60600    je      ntdll! ??
::FNODOBFM::`string'+0×12591 (00000000`7712f02c)
```

So we just need to know the value of RBX and dump the structure to find *OwningThread* field. We can either calculate it from RSP or use **/c** switch with **.frame** command:

```
0: kd> kn
*** Stack trace for last set context - .thread/.cxr resets it
 # Child-SP          RetAddr           Call Site
00 fffff880`0e870940 fffff800`01c76972 nt!KiSwapContext+0x7a
01 fffff880`0e870a80 fffff800`01c87d8f nt!KiCommitThreadWait+0x1d2
02 fffff880`0e870b10 fffff800`01f7b2be nt!KeWaitForSingleObject+0x19f
03 fffff880`0e870bb0 fffff800`01c801d3 nt!NtWaitForSingleObject+0xde
04 fffff880`0e870c20 00000000`773912fa nt!KiSystemServiceCopyEnd+0x13
05 00000000`022ae6c8 00000000`773470b4 ntdll!NtWaitForSingleObject+0xa
06 00000000`022ae6d0 00000000`ff4013a3 ntdll!RtlAcquireResourceShared+0xd0
07 00000000`022ae710 00000000`ff401675
lsm!CAutoSharedLock::CAutoSharedLock+0×61
```

```
08 00000000`022ae7e0 00000000`ff402c68 lsm!CTSSession::getTerminal+0×21
09 00000000`022ae820 000007fe`fd8bff85 lsm!RpcGetEnumResult+0×202
0a 00000000`022ae980 000007fe`fd8b4de2 RPCRT4!Invoke+0×65
0b 00000000`022ae9e0 000007fe`fd8b17bd RPCRT4!NdrStubCall2+0×32a
0c 00000000`022af000 000007fe`fd8b3254 RPCRT4!NdrServerCall2+0×1d
0d 00000000`022af030 000007fe`fd8b33b6 RPCRT4!DispatchToStubInCNoAvrf+0×14
0e 00000000`022af060 000007fe`fd8b3aa9
RPCRT4!RPC_INTERFACE::DispatchToStubWorker+0×146
0f 00000000`022af180 000007fe`fd8b375d RPCRT4!LRPC_SCALL::DispatchRequest+0×149
10 00000000`022af260 000007fe`fd8d09ff RPCRT4!LRPC_SCALL::HandleRequest+0×20d
11 00000000`022af390 000007fe`fd8d05b5 RPCRT4!LRPC_ADDRESS::ProcessIO+0×3bf
12 00000000`022af4d0 00000000`7735b6bb RPCRT4!LrpcIoComplete+0xa5
13 00000000`022af560 00000000`7735ff2f ntdll!TppAlpcpExecuteCallback+0×26b
14 00000000`022af5f0 00000000`7713652d ntdll!TppWorkerThread+0×3f8
15 00000000`022af8f0 00000000`7736c541 kernel32!BaseThreadInitThunk+0xd
16 00000000`022af920 00000000`00000000 ntdll!RtlUserThreadStart+0×1d


0: kd> .frame /c 6
06 00000000`022ae6d0 00000000`ff4013a3
ntdll!RtlAcquireResourceShared+0xd0
rax=0000000000000000 rbx=00000000023ac128 rcx=0000000000000000
rdx=0000000000000000 rsi=0000000077472410 rdi=0000000000000001
rip=00000000773470b4 rsp=00000000022ae6d0 rbp=0000000000000000
r8=0000000000000000  r9=0000000000000000 r10=0000000000000000
r11=0000000000000000 r12=29406b2a1a85bd43 r13=0000000000000009
r14=000000000000000c r15=00000000022aef20
iopl=0         nv up di pl nz na pe nc
cs=0000  ss=0000  ds=0000  es=0000  fs=0000  gs=0000                efl=
00000000
ntdll!RtlAcquireResourceShared+0xd0:
00000000`773470b4 3d02010000      cmp     eax,102h


0: kd> dp rbx+28 L10
00000000`023ac150 00000000`00001244 00000000`000001b5
00000000`023ac160 00000000`00000f3c ffffffff`00000000
00000000`023ac170 00000000`000021a0 00000000`00000000
00000000`023ac180 00000000`02735fc0 00000000`00000001
00000000`023ac190 00000000`00000000 01cf07ac`9fa06d27
00000000`023ac1a0 00000000`00000000 00000000`00000000
00000000`023ac1b0 ffffffff`ffffffff 00000000`00000000
00000000`023ac1c0 00000000`00000000 00000000`00000000
```

We check all these handles (*OwnerThread* seems come earlier with *NumberActive* field missing, but that could just a difference between the old x86 structure implemented in ReactOS and x64 Windows):

```
0: kd> !handle 00000000`00001244


PROCESS fffffa804a16b260
SessionId: 0  Cid: 03c0    Peb: 7fffffdc000  ParentCid: 0350
DirBase: 195950000  ObjectTable: fffff8a0032424e0  HandleCount: 5252.
Image: lsm.exe


Handle table at fffff8a0032424e0 with 5252 entries in use


1244: Object: fffffa804a79ad50  GrantedAccess: 00100003 Entry:
fffff8a022b39910
Object: fffffa804a79ad50  Type: (fffffa8048fc8790) Semaphore
ObjectHeader: fffffa804a79ad20 (new version)
HandleCount: 1  PointerCount: 438


0: kd> !handle 00000000`00000f3c


PROCESS fffffa804a16b260
SessionId: 0  Cid: 03c0    Peb: 7fffffdc000  ParentCid: 0350
DirBase: 195950000  ObjectTable: fffff8a0032424e0  HandleCount: 5252.
Image: lsm.exe


Handle table at fffff8a0032424e0 with 5252 entries in use


0f3c: Object: fffffa804fa81f60  GrantedAccess: 00100003 Entry:
fffff8a02cd3ecf0
Object: fffffa804fa81f60  Type: (fffffa8048fc8790) Semaphore
ObjectHeader: fffffa804fa81f30 (new version)
HandleCount: 1  PointerCount: 1


0: kd> !thread -t 00000000`000021a0 3f
THREAD fffffa804d5d51b0 Cid 03c0.21a0 Teb: 000007fffff9c000 Win32Thread:
0000000000000000 WAIT: (WrLpcReply) UserMode Non-Alertable
fffffa804d5d5578  Semaphore Limit 0×1
Waiting for reply to ALPC Message fffff8a02c9a9500 : queued at port
fffffa804ac4e7d0 : owned by process fffffa804adc8730
Not impersonating
DeviceMap                  fffff8a0000088c0
Owning Process             fffffa804a16b260    Image:       lsm.exe
Attached Process           N/A        Image:       N/A
Wait Start TickCount       73337319   Ticks: 1466453 (0:06:21:53.328)
Context Switch Count       69         IdealProcessor: 1
UserTime                   00:00:00.000
KernelTime                 00:00:00.000
Win32 Start Address ntdll!TppWorkerThread (0×000000007735fbf0)
Stack Init fffff8800aa1fdb0 Current fffff8800aa1f600
Base fffff8800aa20000 Limit fffff8800aa1a000 Call 0
Priority 9 BasePriority 8 UnusualBoost 0 ForegroundBoost 0 IoPriority 2
PagePriority 5
Kernel stack not resident.
```

```
Child-SP          RetAddr           Call Site
fffff880`0aa1f640 fffff800`01c76972 nt!KiSwapContext+0x7a
fffff880`0aa1f780 fffff800`01c87d8f nt!KiCommitThreadWait+0x1d2
fffff880`0aa1f810 fffff800`01ca25af nt!KeWaitForSingleObject+0x19f
fffff880`0aa1f8b0 fffff800`01f968b6 nt!AlpcpSignalAndWait+0x8f
fffff880`0aa1f960 fffff800`01f95fb0 nt!AlpcpReceiveSynchronousReply+0x46
fffff880`0aa1f9c0 fffff800`01f93dab nt!AlpcpProcessSynchronousRequest+0x33d
fffff880`0aa1fb00 fffff800`01c801d3 nt!NtAlpcSendWaitReceivePort+0x1ab
fffff880`0aa1fbb0 00000000`77391b0a nt!KiSystemServiceCopyEnd+0x13 (TrapFrame @
fffff880`0aa1fc20)
00000000`01dddb48 000007fe`fd8c8306 ntdll!ZwAlpcSendWaitReceivePort+0xa
00000000`01dddb50 000007fe`fd8c2a02 RPCRT4!LRPC_CCALL::SendReceive+0x156
00000000`01dddc10 000007fe`ff5b28c0 RPCRT4!I_RpcSendReceive+0x42
00000000`01dddc40 000007fe`ff5b282f ole32!ThreadSendReceive+0x40
[d:\w7rtm\com\ole32\com\dcomrem\channelb.cxx @ 5003]
00000000`01dddc90 000007fe`ff5b265b
ole32!CRpcChannelBuffer::SwitchAptAndDispatchCall+0xa3
[d:\w7rtm\com\ole32\com\dcomrem\channelb.cxx @ 4454]
00000000`01dddd30 000007fe`ff46daaa ole32!CRpcChannelBuffer::SendReceive2+0x11b
[d:\w7rtm\com\ole32\com\dcomrem\channelb.cxx @ 4074]
00000000`01dddef0 000007fe`ff46da0c ole32!CAptRpcChnl::SendReceive+0x52
[d:\w7rtm\com\ole32\com\dcomrem\callctrl.cxx @ 603]
00000000`01dddfc0 000007fe`ff5b205d ole32!CCtxComChnl::SendReceive+0x68
[d:\w7rtm\com\ole32\com\dcomrem\ctxchnl.cxx @ 734]
00000000`01dde070 000007fe`fd96b949 ole32!NdrExtpProxySendReceive+0x45
[d:\w7rtm\com\rpc\ndrole\proxy.cxx @ 1932]
00000000`01dde0a0 000007fe`ff5b21d0 RPCRT4!NdrpClientCall3+0x2e2
00000000`01dde360 000007fe`ff46d8a2 ole32!ObjectStublessClient+0x11d
[d:\w7rtm\com\rpc\ndrole\amd64\stblsclt.cxx @ 621]
00000000`01dde6f0 00000000`ff417d26 ole32!ObjectStubless+0x42
[d:\w7rtm\com\rpc\ndrole\amd64\stubless.asm @ 117]
00000000`01dde740 00000000`ff4186ba lsm!CTSSession::Disconnect+0x3a5
00000000`01dde810 000007fe`fd8bff85 lsm!RpcDisconnect+0x15e
00000000`01dde850 000007fe`fd96b68e RPCRT4!Invoke+0x65
00000000`01dde8a0 000007fe`fd8a92e0 RPCRT4!Ndr64StubWorker+0x61b
00000000`01ddee60 000007fe`fd8b3254 RPCRT4!NdrServerCallAll+0x40
00000000`01ddeeb0 000007fe`fd8b33b6 RPCRT4!DispatchToStubInCNoAvrf+0x14
00000000`01ddeee0 000007fe`fd8b3aa9
RPCRT4!RPC_INTERFACE::DispatchToStubWorker+0x146
00000000`01ddf000 000007fe`fd8b375d RPCRT4!LRPC_SCALL::DispatchRequest+0x149
00000000`01ddf0e0 000007fe`fd8d09ff RPCRT4!LRPC_SCALL::HandleRequest+0x20d
00000000`01ddf210 000007fe`fd8d05b5 RPCRT4!LRPC_ADDRESS::ProcessIO+0x3bf
00000000`01ddf350 00000000`7735b6bb RPCRT4!LrpcIoComplete+0xa5
00000000`01ddf3e0 00000000`7735ff2f ntdll!TppAlpcpExecuteCallback+0x26b
00000000`01ddf470 00000000`7713652d ntdll!TppWorkerThread+0x3f8
00000000`01ddf770 00000000`7736c541 kernel32!BaseThreadInitThunk+0xd
00000000`01ddf7a0 00000000`00000000 ntdll!RtlUserThreadStart+0x1d
```

We see the wait chain continues with waiting for an ALPC request (Volume 3, page 97).

Memory Fluctuation (Process Heap)

In process heap **Memory Leak** (Volume 1, page 356) pattern we recommended acquiring sequential memory dumps spaced by 100MB. Unfortunately customers may send memory dumps spaced more closely, say by 10 - 20 MB or less after memory consumption growth already started sometime in the past, for example, when they feel further process growth may impact their system performance. The analysis of process heap from memory dumps with enabled user mode stack database and corresponding UMDH log differences may show only **Memory Fluctuation**, where memory increases for specific stack trace allocations may follow by decreases or by small increases (S_i is for memory dump size [horizontal bars], t_i is for memory acquisition time):

M, KB

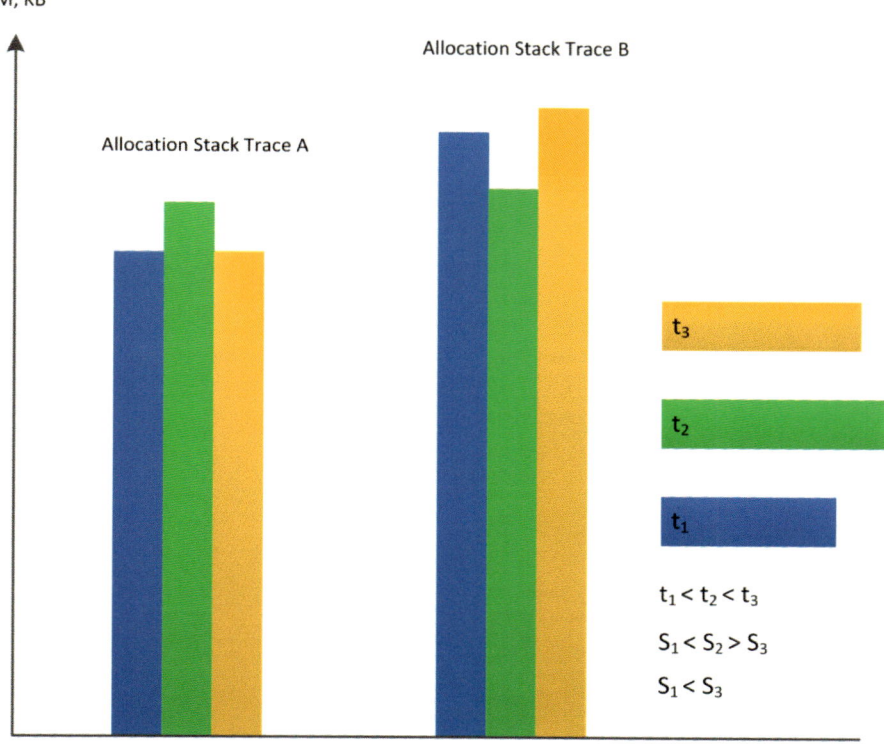

In such cases, it is difficult to choose among various local memory fluctuations to continue the further investigation. However, a baseline process memory dump, for example, just after process start, helps to choose which stack trace allocations investigate first: those having bigger absolute memory allocation increase (Allocation Stack Trace B):

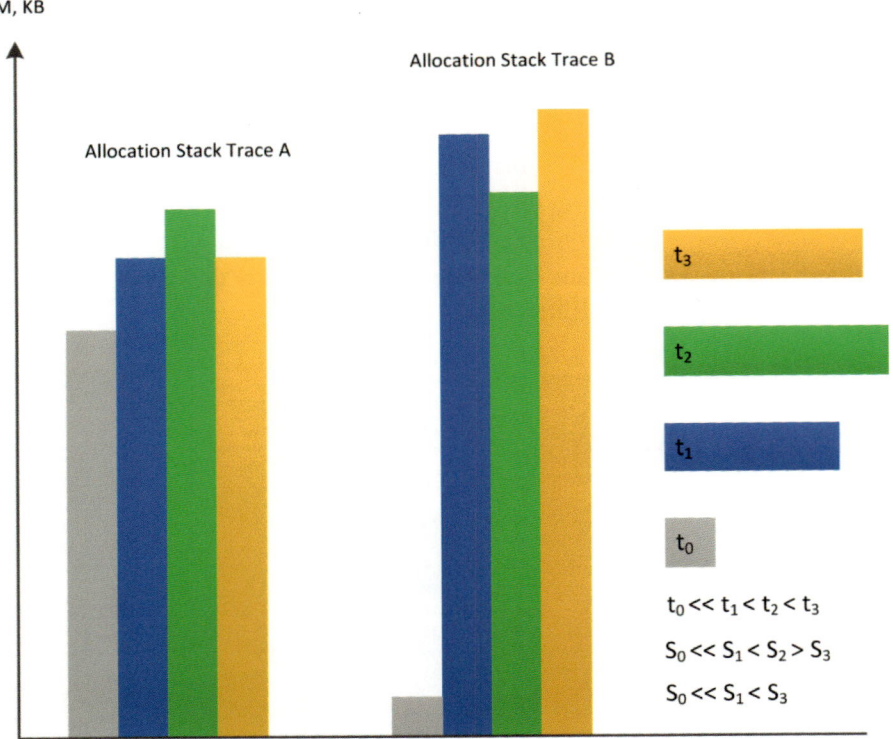

$$t_0 \ll t_1 < t_2 < t_3$$
$$S_0 \ll S_1 < S_2 > S_3$$
$$S_0 \ll S_1 < S_3$$

Last Object

Although in the case of system hangs we, usually, recommend dumping **Stack Trace Collection** (Volume 1, page 409), in some cases it is very time-consuming, especially when it involves thousands of processes such as in modern terminal services environments. In such a case, if the problem description indicates the last action such as a not progressing user logon or a recently launched process we first check the tail of the corresponding linked list where **Last Object** is usually added to the tail of the list:

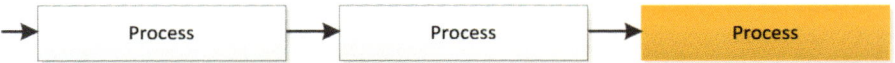

Sometimes we can simply check the end of some enumerated collection, such as sessions (dotted lines represent ALPC **Wait Chains**, Volume 3, page 97):

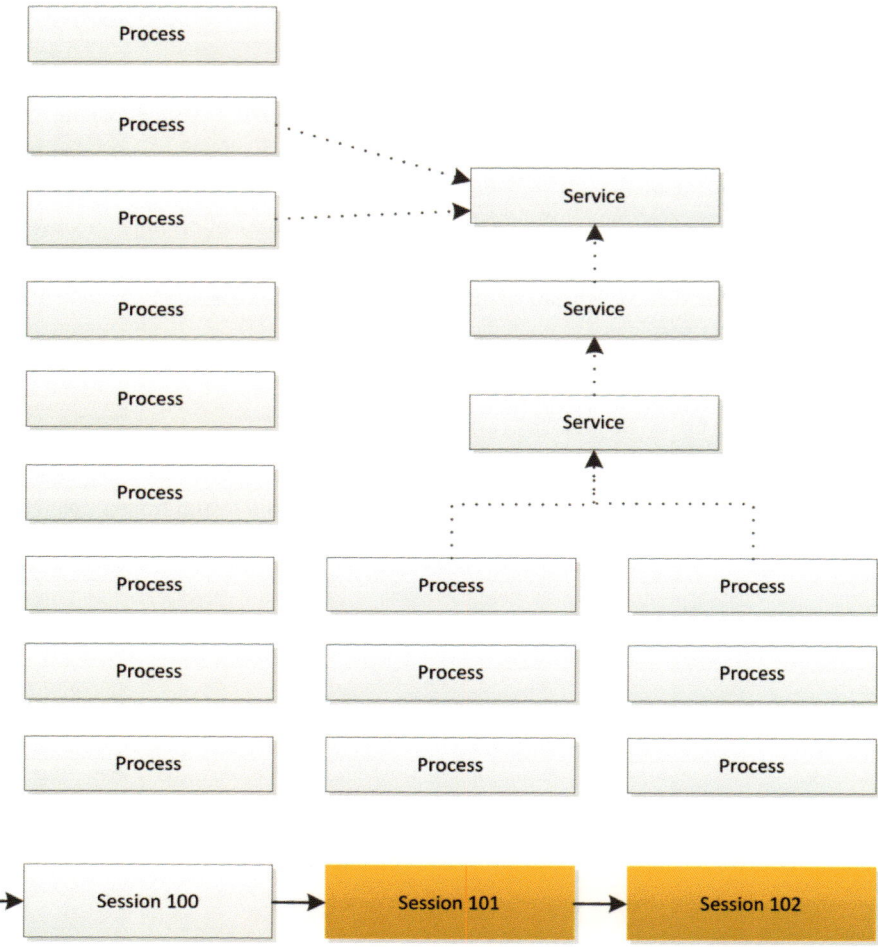

This analysis pattern can be added to the first tier of RSDP (Volume 7, page 444). If nothing found around a couple of **Last Objects,** we then resort to the analysis of entire linked lists.

Rough Stack Trace

This pattern is an example of more general **Execution Residue** (Volume 2, page 239) pattern or **Caller-n-Callee** (Volume 6, page 138) for managed space. It is just a collection of symbolic references (may also include **Coincidental Symbolic Information**, Volume 1, page 390) from the thread stack region or its fragment. In WinDbg, we can get it by using **dpS** command:

```
0:003> !teb
TEB at 000007fffffd6000
ExceptionList:        0000000000000000
StackBase:            0000000002450000
StackLimit:           000000000244b000
SubSystemTib:         0000000000000000
FiberData:            0000000000001e00
ArbitraryUserPointer: 0000000000000000
Self:                 000007fffffd6000
EnvironmentPointer:   0000000000000000
ClientId:             00000000000047fc . 0000000000004824
RpcHandle:            0000000000000000
Tls Storage:          000007fffffd6058
PEB Address:          000007fffffda000
LastErrorValue:       0
LastStatusValue:      c0000302
Count Owned Locks:    0
HardErrorMode:        0


0:003> dpS 000000000244b000 0000000002450000
000007fe`fd4a8a2e ole32!InternalVerifyStackAvailable+0x44
[d:\winmain\minio\safealloca\alloca.c @ 317]
000007fe`fd4a8a2e ole32!InternalVerifyStackAvailable+0x44
[d:\winmain\minio\safealloca\alloca.c @ 317]
000007fe`fd4a8a2e ole32!InternalVerifyStackAvailable+0x44
[d:\winmain\minio\safealloca\alloca.c @ 317]
00000000`771d5430 ntdll!RtlpInterceptorRoutines
00000000`771134d8 ntdll!RtlAllocateHeap+0x16c
00000000`770ec9c3 ntdll!RtlAppendUnicodeStringToString+0x53
00000000`76eaebe5 kernel32!Wow64RedirectKeyPathInternal+0x2b7
00000000`770ec9c3 ntdll!RtlAppendUnicodeStringToString+0x53
00000000`771140fd ntdll!RtlFreeHeap+0x1a6
00000000`76eaec01 kernel32!ConstructKernelKeyPath+0x15f
00000000`76eaedd3 kernel32!Wow64NtOpenKey+0xee
00000000`771140fd ntdll!RtlFreeHeap+0x1a6
00000000`76ebc8aa kernel32!BaseRegOpenClassKeyFromLocation+0x3ba
00000000`76f3edf0 kernel32!`string'
00000000`771d5430 ntdll!RtlpInterceptorRoutines
00000000`76ebc9b9 kernel32!BaseRegGetUserPrefixLength+0xea
00000000`76f3ee38 kernel32!`string'
00000000`76f3edc8 kernel32!`string'
00000000`76ebc3a8 kernel32!BaseRegGetKeySemantics+0x1b8
00000000`771150d3 ntdll!RtlNtStatusToDosError+0x27
00000000`76eb36b7 kernel32!LocalBaseRegOpenKey+0x276
000007fe`fd4b6c79 ole32!GetUnquotedPath+0x29
[d:\w7rtm\com\ole32\com\objact\dllcache.cxx @ 2256]
```

```
000007fe`fd4b7019
ole32!CClassCache::CDllPathEntry::NegotiateDllInstantiationProperties2+0x145
[d:\w7rtm\com\ole32\com\objact\dllcache.cxx @ 3092]
00000000`771d5430 ntdll!RtlpInterceptorRoutines
00000000`771134d8 ntdll!RtlAllocateHeap+0x16c
00000000`77115cc4 ntdll!RtlpAllocateHeap+0xc12
000007fe`fdc10359 usp10!CUspShapingClient::AllocMem+0x49
000007fe`fdc48942 usp10!COtlsClient::AllocMem+0x12
000007fe`fdc48942 usp10!COtlsClient::AllocMem+0x12
000007fe`fdc1d4f1 usp10!UspFreeMem+0x61
000007fe`fdc4896e usp10!COtlsClient::FreeMem+0xe
000007fe`fdc6e817 usp10!ApplyFeatures+0xa17
000007fe`fdc6f2f2 usp10!ApplyLookup+0x592
000007fe`fdc48901 usp10!COtlsClient::GetDefaultGlyphs+0x131
000007fe`fdc60100 usp10!HangulEngineGetGlyphs+0x2c0
000007fe`fdc10359 usp10!CUspShapingClient::AllocMem+0x49
000007fe`fdc48942 usp10!COtlsClient::AllocMem+0x12
000007fe`fdc10359 usp10!CUspShapingClient::AllocMem+0x49
000007fe`fdc1d4f1 usp10!UspFreeMem+0x61
000007fe`fdc48942 usp10!COtlsClient::AllocMem+0x12
000007fe`fdc1d4f1 usp10!UspFreeMem+0x61
000007fe`fdc4896e usp10!COtlsClient::FreeMem+0xe
000007fe`fdc6e817 usp10!ApplyFeatures+0xa17
000007fe`fdc6aaa8 usp10!RePositionOtlGlyphs+0x238
000007fe`fdc48901 usp10!COtlsClient::GetDefaultGlyphs+0x131
000007fe`fdc60100 usp10!HangulEngineGetGlyphs+0x2c0
000007fe`fdc48798 usp10!COtlsClient::ReleaseOtlTable+0x78
000007fe`fdc6ae85 usp10!otlResourceMgr::detach+0xc5
00000000`7717c63e ntdll!EtwEventWriteNoRegistration+0xae
000007fe`fdc48a99 usp10!COtlsClient::Release+0x49
00000000`771150d3 ntdll!RtlNtStatusToDosError+0x27
00000000`7716bd85 ntdll!WaitForWerSvc+0x85
00000000`7717b94e ntdll!WerpAllocateAndInitializeSid+0xbe
00000000`7716bd90 ntdll! ?? ::FNODOBFM::`string'
00000000`77175dcf ntdll!WerpFreeSid+0x3f
00000000`7718123d ntdll!SendMessageToWERService+0x22d
00000000`77181260 ntdll! ?? ::FNODOBFM::`string'
00000000`77182308 ntdll!ReportExceptionInternal+0xc8
000007fe`fd061430 KERNELBASE!WaitForMultipleObjectsEx+0xe8
00000000`76ec1723 kernel32!WaitForMultipleObjectsExImplementation+0xb3
00000000`76f3b5e5 kernel32!WerpReportFaultInternal+0x215
00000000`76f3b767 kernel32!WerpReportFault+0x77
00000000`76f3b7bf kernel32!BasepReportFault+0x1f
00000000`76f3b9dc kernel32!UnhandledExceptionFilter+0x1fc
00000000`77118d7e ntdll!RtlpFindUnicodeStringInSection+0x50e
00000000`771198fc ntdll!LdrpFindLoadedDll+0x10c
00000000`770e9caa ntdll!RtlDecodePointer+0x2a
00000000`770c0000 ntdll!RtlDeactivateActivationContext <PERF> (ntdll+0x0)
00000000`771e8180 ntdll!`string'+0xc040
00000000`771e818c ntdll!`string'+0xc04c
00000000`77153398 ntdll! ?? ::FNODOBFM::`string'+0x2365
00000000`770d85c8 ntdll!_C_specific_handler+0x8c
00000000`770c0000 ntdll!RtlDeactivateActivationContext <PERF> (ntdll+0x0)
00000000`770ec541 ntdll!RtlUserThreadStart+0x1d
00000000`770e9d2d ntdll!RtlpExecuteHandlerForException+0xd
00000000`77202dd0 ntdll!CsrPortMemoryRemoteDelta <PERF> (ntdll+0x142dd0)
00000000`770d91cf ntdll!RtlDispatchException+0x45a
00000000`76fadda0 kernel32!__PchSym_ <PERF> (kernel32+0x10dda0)
00000000`7711920a ntdll!RtlDosApplyFileIsolationRedirection_Ustr+0x3da
00000000`77202dd0 ntdll!CsrPortMemoryRemoteDelta <PERF> (ntdll+0x142dd0)
```

```
00000000`771e8180 ntdll!`string'+0xc040
00000000`770c0000 ntdll!RtlDeactivateActivationContext <PERF> (ntdll+0x0)
00000000`770ec541 ntdll!RtlUserThreadStart+0x1d
00000000`770c0000 ntdll!RtlDeactivateActivationContext <PERF> (ntdll+0x0)
00000000`77202dd0 ntdll!CsrPortMemoryRemoteDelta <PERF> (ntdll+0x142dd0)
00000000`771d7718 ntdll!LdrpDefaultExtension
00000000`770d852c ntdll!_C_specific_handler
00000000`771e8180 ntdll!`string'+0xc040
000007fe`ff3625c0 msctf!s_szCompClassName
000007fe`fd602790 ole32!`string'
00000000`770e7a33 ntdll!LdrpFindOrMapDll+0x138
00000000`771192a8 ntdll!LdrpApplyFileNameRedirection+0x2d3
000007fe`fd602848 ole32!`string'
00000000`771d5430 ntdll!RtlpInterceptorRoutines
00000000`77113448 ntdll!RtlAllocateHeap+0xe4
00000000`76fd88b8 user32!GetPropW+0x4d
00000000`76fd88b8 user32!GetPropW+0x4d
00000000`76fd7931 user32!IsWindow+0x9
00000000`76fd7931 user32!IsWindow+0x9
00000000`770f41c8 ntdll!RtlpReAllocateHeap+0x178
000007fe`fb601381 uxtheme!CThemeWnd::_PreDefWindowProc+0x31
00000000`76eb59e0 kernel32!BaseThreadInitThunk
00000000`ffdbdb32 calc!CTimedCalc::Start+0xa9
00000000`ffd90000 calc!CCalculatorController::CCalculatorController <PERF>
(calc+0x0)
00000000`ffe0ac64 calc!_dyn_tls_init_callback <PERF> (calc+0x7ac64)
00000000`76ea0000 kernel32!TestResourceDataMatchEntry <PERF> (kernel32+0x0)
00000000`76fadda0 kernel32!__PchSym_ <PERF> (kernel32+0x10dda0)
00000000`770c0000 ntdll!RtlDeactivateActivationContext <PERF> (ntdll+0x0)
00000000`77202dd0 ntdll!CsrPortMemoryRemoteDelta <PERF> (ntdll+0x142dd0)
00000000`76fd760e user32!RealDefWindowProcW+0x5a
000007fe`fb600037 uxtheme!operator delete <PERF> (uxtheme+0x37)
00000000`77111248 ntdll!KiUserExceptionDispatch+0x2e
000007fe`fb63fb40 uxtheme!$$VProc_ImageExportDirectory
00000000`ffdbdb27 calc!CTimedCalc::WatchDogThread+0xb2
00000000`76fe76c2 user32!DefDlgProcW+0x36
00000000`76fd9bef user32!UserCallWinProcCheckWow+0x1cb
00000000`76fd9b43 user32!UserCallWinProcCheckWow+0x99
00000000`76fd9bef user32!UserCallWinProcCheckWow+0x1cb
00000000`76fd72cb user32!DispatchClientMessage+0xc3
00000000`770e46b4 ntdll!NtdllDialogWndProc_W
00000000`ffdbdb27 calc!CTimedCalc::WatchDogThread+0xb2
00000000`ffdbdb27 calc!CTimedCalc::WatchDogThread+0xb2
00000000`77101530 ntdll!NtdllDispatchMessage_W
00000000`76fe505b user32!DialogBox2+0x2ec
00000000`ffd90000 calc!CCalculatorController::CCalculatorController <PERF>
(calc+0x0)
00000000`76fe4edd user32!InternalDialogBox+0x135
00000000`ffdcedb0 calc!CTimedCalc::TimeOutDlgProc
00000000`ffdcedb0 calc!CTimedCalc::TimeOutDlgProc
00000000`ffd90000 calc!CCalculatorController::CCalculatorController <PERF>
(calc+0x0)
00000000`76fe4f52 user32!DialogBoxIndirectParamAorW+0x58
00000000`ffdcedb0 calc!CTimedCalc::TimeOutDlgProc
00000000`ffdcedb0 calc!CTimedCalc::TimeOutDlgProc
00000000`ffd90000 calc!CCalculatorController::CCalculatorController <PERF>
(calc+0x0)
00000000`76fdd476 user32!DialogBoxParamW+0x66
00000000`ffdcedb0 calc!CTimedCalc::TimeOutDlgProc
00000000`ffdbdafa calc!CTimedCalc::WatchDogThread+0x72
```

```
00000000`76eb59ed kernel32!BaseThreadInitThunk+0xd
00000000`770ec541 ntdll!RtlUserThreadStart+0x1d
00000000`76f3b7e0 kernel32!UnhandledExceptionFilter
00000000`76f3b7e0 kernel32!UnhandledExceptionFilter
```

The name for this pattern comes from rough sets[7] in mathematics.

---

[7] http://en.wikipedia.org/wiki/Rough_set

Past Stack Trace

When we look at a stack trace in a memory dump, we see only the current thread execution snapshot of function calls. Consider this stack trace, for example, from **Spiking Thread** (Volume 1, page 305):

```
0:000> k
Child-SP RetAddr   Call Site
00000000`0012d010 00000000`76eb59ed App!WinMain+0x1eda
00000000`0012f7c0 00000000`770ec541 kernel32!BaseThreadInitThunk+0xd
00000000`0012f7f0 00000000`00000000 ntdll!RtlUserThreadStart+0x1d
```

By looking at **Rough Stack Trace** (page 39) we may be able to reconstruct **Past Stack Trace** of what had happened just before the memory snapshot was taken:

```
0:000> k
Child-SP RetAddr   Call Site
00000000`0012cfd8 00000000`76fd9e9e user32!ZwUserGetMessage+0xa
00000000`0012cfe0 00000000`ffd91a8c user32!GetMessageW+0x34
00000000`0012d010 00000000`76eb59ed App!WinMain+0x1dca
00000000`0012f7c0 00000000`770ec541 kernel32!BaseThreadInitThunk+0xd
00000000`0012f7f0 00000000`00000000 ntdll!RtlUserThreadStart+0x1d
```

The stack region "time" zones are illustrated by the following picture:

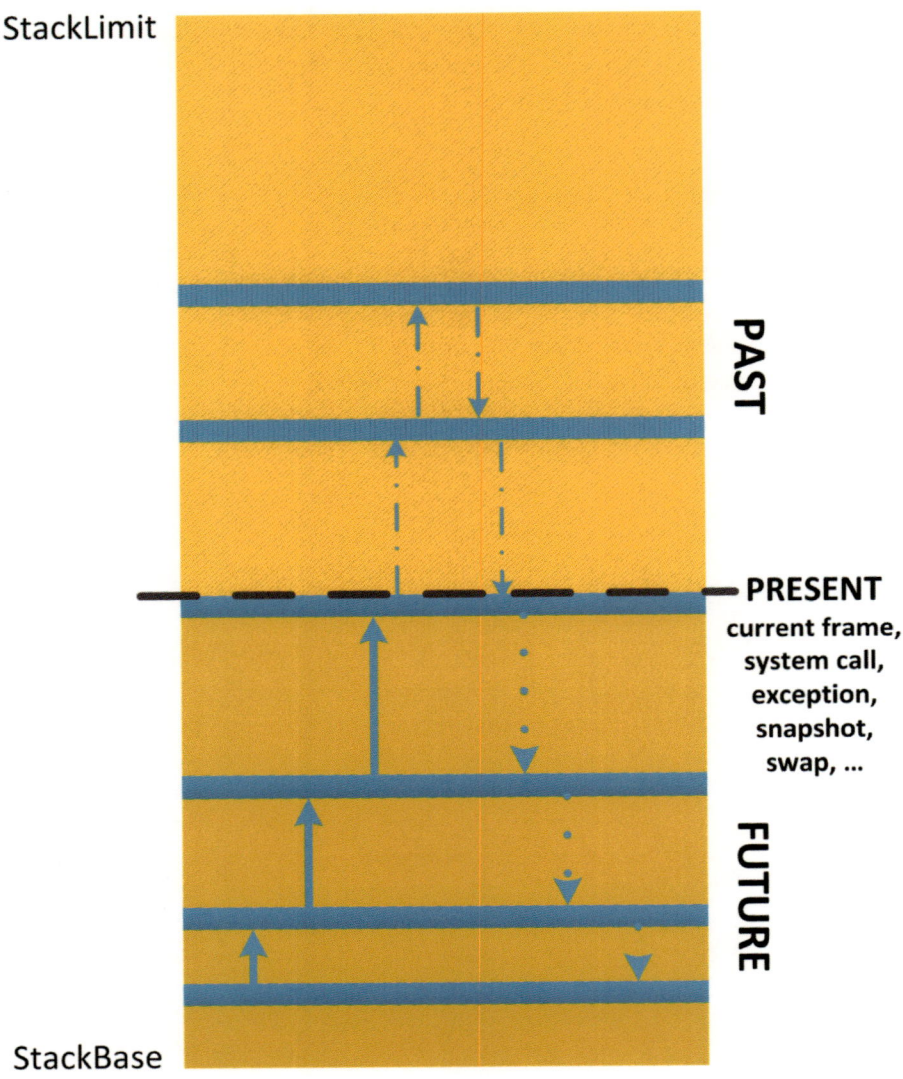

The "Future" zone takes its name from the not yet executed returns. Of course, each stack subtrace generates its own partition. A similar version of this pattern was first introduced in Debugging TV Frames episode 0×24. You can watch the video[8] and find source code, WinDbg logs, and presentation on Debugging TV website[9].

---

[8] https://www.youtube.com/watch?v=qRaabDzW3ww

[9] http://www.debugging.tv/

Stack Trace (I/O Request)

If a thread has an associated I/O Request Packet (IRP) we may see another type of a stack trace we call **I/O Request Stack Trace**. It also grows bottom-up as can be seen on the diagram #3 (Volume 1, page 701). We can see this stack trace by using **!irp** WinDbg command:

```
0: kd> !thread fffffa801827a4c0 3f
THREAD fffffa801827a4c0 Cid 06c0.50cc Teb: 000007ffffec8000
Win32Thread: fffff900c1c64010 WAIT: (Executive) KernelMode Alertable
fffffa8016f64028 SynchronizationEvent
IRP List:
fffffa80162aa230: (0006,03a0) Flags: 00000884 Mdl: 00000000
[...]
nt!KiSwapContext+0×7a
nt!KiCommitThreadWait+0×1d2
nt!KeWaitForSingleObject+0×19f
nt!FsRtlCancellableWaitForMultipleObjects+0×5e
nt!FsRtlCancellableWaitForSingleObject+0×27
fltmgr! ?? ::FNODOBFM::`string'+0×2bfa
fltmgr!FltpCreate+0×2a9
nt!IopParseDevice+0×14d3
nt!ObpLookupObjectName+0×588
nt!ObOpenObjectByName+0×306
nt!IopCreateFile+0×2bc
nt!NtCreateFile+0×78
nt!KiSystemServiceCopyEnd+0×13
ntdll!NtCreateFile+0xa
[...]

0: kd> !irp fffffa80162aa230
Irp is active with 10 stacks 10 is current (= 0xfffffa80162aa588)
No Mdl: No System Buffer: Thread fffffa801827a4c0: Irp stack trace.
cmd flg cl Device File Completion-Context
[ 0, 0] 0 0 00000000 00000000 00000000-00000000

Args: 00000000 00000000 00000000 00000000
[ 0, 0] 0 0 00000000 00000000 00000000-00000000

Args: 00000000 00000000 00000000 00000000
[ 0, 0] 0 0 00000000 00000000 00000000-00000000

Args: 00000000 00000000 00000000 00000000
[ 0, 0] 0 0 00000000 00000000 00000000-00000000

Args: 00000000 00000000 00000000 00000000
[ 0, 0] 0 0 00000000 00000000 00000000-00000000
```

```
Args: 00000000 00000000 00000000 00000000
[ 0, 0] 0 0 00000000 00000000 00000000-00000000

Args: 00000000 00000000 00000000 00000000
[ 0, 0] 0 0 00000000 00000000 00000000-00000000

Args: 00000000 00000000 00000000 00000000
[ 0, 0] 0 0 00000000 00000000 00000000-00000000

Args: 00000000 00000000 00000000 00000000
[ 0, 0] 0 0 fffffa800cb28030 00000000 fffff880012048f0-
fffffa8016f64010
\FileSystem\Ntfs fltmgr!FltpSynchronizedOperationCompletion
Args: 00000000 00000000 00000000 00000000
>[ 0, 0] 0 1 fffffa800ca00890 fffffa801060d070 00000000-00000000
pending
\FileSystem\FltMgr
Args: fffff88014450868 02000060 00000006 00000000
```

We see the current stack trace pointer points to the bottom I/O stack location. Non-empty top locations are analogous to **Past Stack Trace** (page 43). Further exploration of *Device* and *File* column information may point to further troubleshooting directions such as the **Blocking File** (Volume 6, page 105) pattern example.

By analogy with **Stack Trace Collection** (Volume 1, page 409) pattern that dumps stack traces from all threads based on memory dump type there is also **I/O Stack Trace Collection** (Volume 7, page 101) pattern that dumps I/O request stack traces from all IRPs that were possible to find.

Stack Trace (File System Filters)

Sometimes threads related to file system operations may be **Blocked** (Volume 2, page 184) with not easily recognizable 3rd-party **Top Module** (Volume 6, page 62) with only OS vendor modules such as *NTFS* or *fltmgr* present:

```
nt!KiSwapContext+0x7a
nt!KiCommitThreadWait+0x1d2
nt!KeWaitForSingleObject+0x19f
nt!FsRtlCancellableWaitForMultipleObjects+0x5e
nt!FsRtlCancellableWaitForSingleObject+0x27
fltmgr! ?? ::FNODOBFM::`string'+0x2bfa
fltmgr!FltpCreate+0x2a9
nt!IopParseDevice+0x14d3
nt!ObpLookupObjectName+0x588
nt!ObOpenObjectByName+0x306
nt!IopCreateFile+0x2bc
nt!NtCreateFile+0x78
nt!KiSystemServiceCopyEnd+0x13
ntdll!NtCreateFile+0xa
[...]
```

We see the same modules in **I/O Request Stack Trace** (page 46) from the thread IRP. However, because we see filter manager involved, there may be some 3rd-party file system filters involved. Such filters are called before a device processes a request and also upon the completion of the request. There may be different filter callbacks registered for each case, and they form a similar structure like I/O stack locations (we call this pattern **Filter Stack Trace**):

I/O Stack Trace

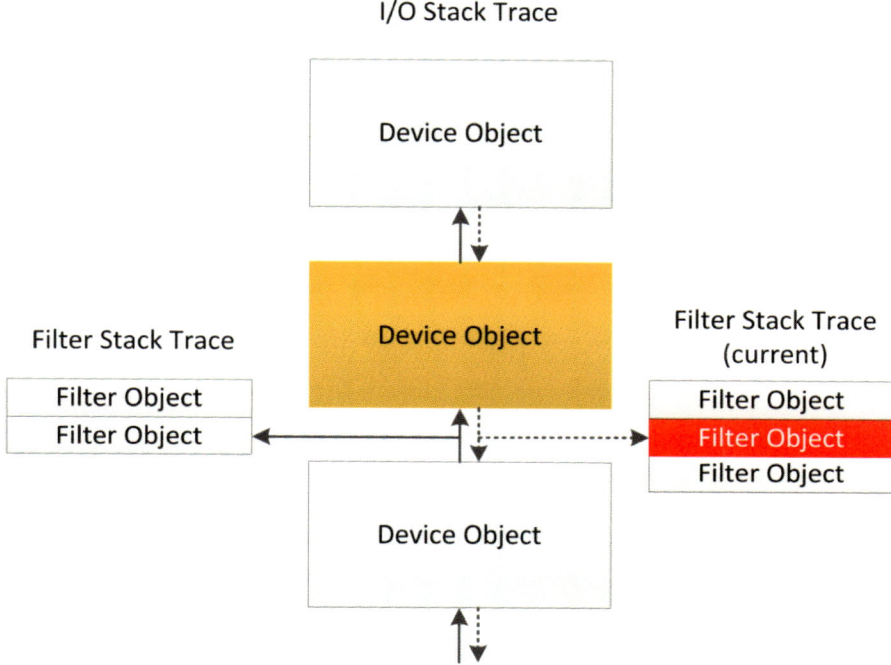

If one of such filters is blocked in a wait chain, this may not be visible on I/O request or thread stacks because of possible asynchronous processing. However, we may use **!fltkd.irpctrl** debugging extension command to examine the IRP context:

```
0: kd> !irp fffffa80162aa230
cmd flg cl Device File Completion-Context
[...]
[ 0, 0] 0 0 fffffa800cb28030 00000000 fffff880012048f0-fffffa8016f64010
\FileSystem\Ntfs fltmgr!FltpSynchronizedOperationCompletion
Args: 00000000 00000000 00000000 00000000
> [ 0, 0] 0 1 fffffa800ca00890 fffffa801060d070 00000000-00000000 pending
\FileSystem\FltMgr
Args: fffff88014450868 02000060 00000006 00000000


0: kd> !fltkd.irpctrl fffffa8016f64010
[...]
Cmd IrpFl OpFl CmpFl Instance FileObjt Completion-Context Node Adr
--------- -------- ----- ----- -------- -------- ------------------ --------
[0,0] 00000884 00 0000 fffffa800d29c010 fffffa801060d070 fffff8800518b474-
0000000000000000 fffffa8016f641e0
("luafv","luafv") luafv!LuafvPostCreate
Args: fffff88014450868 0000000002000060 0000000000000006 0000000000000000
0000000000000000 0000000000000000
>[0,0] 00000884 00 0000 fffffa800e8051d0 fffffa801060d070 fffff88006808440-
0000000000000000 fffffa8016f64160
```

```
("3rdPartyFilter","3rdPartyFilter Instance")
FilterA!FltDriver_PostOperationCallback
Args: fffff88014450868 0000000002000060 0000000000000006 0000000000000000
0000000000000000 0000000000000000
[...]
```

So we see that *FilterA* module may be involved in blocking the thread. We may consider this as **Blocking Module** (Volume 6, page 54) pattern extended to I/O request and filter stack traces.

Stack Trace (Database)

Some troubleshooting and debugging techniques involve saving in some region in memory, called stack trace database, every **Stack Trace** (Volume 1, page 395) that leads to a specific action such as a memory allocation of opening of a resource handle. Typical pattern usage examples include **Process Heap Memory Leak** (Volume 1, page 356), **Insufficient Memory** (Volume 1, page 327) due to **Handle Leak** (Volume 7, page 164). Typical entry in such a database consists of return addresses saved during function calls (that may be **Truncated Stack Trace**, Volume 6, page 86):

```
00000000`00325da0 000007fe`fd5e37aa KERNELBASE!InitializeCriticalSectionAndSpinCount+0xa
00000000`00325da8 00000001`3fd72239 AllocFree!_ioinit+0x2cd
00000000`00325db0 00000001`3fd71115 AllocFree!__tmainCRTStartup+0xc5
00000000`00325db8 00000000`773759ed kernel32!BaseThreadInitThunk+0xd
00000000`00325dc0 00000000`774ac541 ntdll!RtlUserThreadStart+0x1d


0:001> ub 00000001`3fd72239
AllocFree!_ioinit+0x2af:
00000001`3fd7221b cmp eax,3
00000001`3fd7221e jne AllocFree!_ioinit+0x2be (00000001`3fd7222a)
00000001`3fd72220 movsx eax,byte ptr [rbx+8]
00000001`3fd72224 or eax,8
00000001`3fd72227 mov byte ptr [rbx+8],al
00000001`3fd7222a lea rcx,[rbx+10h]
00000001`3fd7222e mov edx,0FA0h
00000001`3fd72233 call qword ptr [AllocFree!_imp_InitializeCriticalSectionAndSpinCount
(00000001`3fd78090)]
```

This slightly differs from 'k'-style stack trace format where the return address belongs to the function on the next line if moving downwards:

```
0:000> k
Child-SP RetAddr Call Site
00000000`002ff9f8 000007fe`fd5e1203 ntdll!ZwDelayExecution+0xa
00000000`002ffa00 00000001`3fd71018 KERNELBASE!SleepEx+0xab
00000000`002ffaa0 00000001`3fd71194 AllocFree!wmain+0x18
00000000`002ffad0 00000000`773759ed AllocFree!__tmainCRTStartup+0x144
00000000`002ffb10 00000000`774ac541 kernel32!BaseThreadInitThunk+0xd
00000000`002ffb40 00000000`00000000 ntdll!RtlUserThreadStart+0x1d


0:000> ub 00000001`3fd71194
AllocFree!__tmainCRTStartup+0x11b:
00000001`3fd7116b je    AllocFree!__tmainCRTStartup+0x124 (00000001`3fd71174)
00000001`3fd7116d mov   ecx,eax
00000001`3fd7116f call  AllocFree!_amsg_exit (00000001`3fd718ec)
00000001`3fd71174 mov   r8,qword ptr [AllocFree!_wenviron (00000001`3fd80868)]
00000001`3fd7117b mov   qword ptr [AllocFree!__winitenv (00000001`3fd80890)],r8
00000001`3fd71182 mov   rdx,qword ptr [AllocFree!__wargv (00000001`3fd80858)]
00000001`3fd71189 mov   ecx,dword ptr [AllocFree!__argc (00000001`3fd8084c)]
00000001`3fd7118f call  AllocFree!wmain (00000001`3fd71000)
```

Sometimes we can see such traces as **Execution Residue** (Volume 2, page 239) inside a stack or some other region. If user mode stack trace database is enabled in *gflags.exe* we might be able to dump the specific database region:

```
0:001> !gflag
Current NtGlobalFlag contents: 0x00001000
ust - Create user mode stack trace database


0:001> !address
[...]
BaseAddress EndAddress+1 RegionSize Type        State      Protect      Usage
-------------------------------------------------------------------------------------------
---------
[...]
+ 0`00300000 0`00326000   0`00026000 MEM_PRIVATE MEM_COMMIT  PAGE_READWRITE Other [Stack Trace Database]
0`00326000 0`01aff000   0`017d9000 MEM_PRIVATE MEM_RESERVE              Other [Stack Trace Database]
0`01aff000 0`01b00000   0`00001000 MEM_PRIVATE MEM_COMMIT  PAGE_READWRITE Other [Stack Trace Database]
[...]


0:001> dps 0`00326000-1000 0`00326000
[...]
00000000`003257e0 00000000`00000000
00000000`003257e8 00030001`00001801
00000000`003257f0 00000000`774c34eb ntdll!LdrpInitializeProcess+0x7e6
00000000`003257f8 00000000`774c1937 ntdll! ?? ::FNODOBFM::`string'+0x28ff0
00000000`00325800 00000000`774ac34e ntdll!LdrInitializeThunk+0xe
00000000`00325808 00000000`00000000
00000000`00325810 00000000`00000000
00000000`00325818 00030002`00001801
00000000`00325820 00000000`774c3511 ntdll!LdrpInitializeProcess+0x80c
00000000`00325828 00000000`774c1937 ntdll! ?? ::FNODOBFM::`string'+0x28ff0
00000000`00325830 00000000`774ac34e ntdll!LdrInitializeThunk+0xe
00000000`00325838 00000000`00000000
00000000`00325840 00000000`00000000
00000000`00325848 00040003`00001801
00000000`00325850 00000000`774bda86 ntdll!RtlCreateHeap+0x506
00000000`00325858 00000000`774c3557 ntdll!LdrpInitializeProcess+0x851
00000000`00325860 00000000`774c1937 ntdll! ?? ::FNODOBFM::`string'+0x28ff0
00000000`00325868 00000000`774ac34e ntdll!LdrInitializeThunk+0xe
00000000`00325870 00000000`00000000
00000000`00325878 00050004`00002801
00000000`00325880 00000000`7751998a ntdll! ?? ::FNODOBFM::`string'+0xdc1a
00000000`00325888 00000000`774bdaee ntdll!RtlCreateHeap+0x56e
00000000`00325890 00000000`774c3557 ntdll!LdrpInitializeProcess+0x851
00000000`00325898 00000000`774c1937 ntdll! ?? ::FNODOBFM::`string'+0x28ff0
00000000`003258a0 00000000`774ac34e ntdll!LdrInitializeThunk+0xe
00000000`003258a8 00000000`00000000
00000000`003258b0 00000000`00000000
00000000`003258b8 00030005`00001801
00000000`003258c0 00000000`774c359e ntdll!LdrpInitializeProcess+0x902
00000000`003258c8 00000000`774c1937 ntdll! ?? ::FNODOBFM::`string'+0x28ff0
00000000`003258d0 00000000`774ac34e ntdll!LdrInitializeThunk+0xe
00000000`003258d8 00000000`00000000
00000000`003258e0 00000000`00000000
00000000`003258e8 00030006`00001801
00000000`003258f0 00000000`774c35af ntdll!LdrpInitializeProcess+0x913
00000000`003258f8 00000000`774c1937 ntdll! ?? ::FNODOBFM::`string'+0x28ff0
00000000`00325900 00000000`774ac34e ntdll!LdrInitializeThunk+0xe
00000000`00325908 00000000`00000000
```

```
00000000`00325910 00000000`00000000
00000000`00325918 00090007`00004801
00000000`00325920 00000000`774bda86 ntdll!RtlCreateHeap+0×506
00000000`00325928 00000000`774c47ff ntdll!CsrpConnectToServer+0×41f
00000000`00325930 00000000`774c43c5 ntdll!CsrClientConnectToServer+0×230
00000000`00325938 000007fe`fd5ee232 KERNELBASE!KernelBaseDllInitialize+0×148
00000000`00325940 00000000`774bb108 ntdll!LdrpRunInitializeRoutines+0×1fe
00000000`00325948 00000000`774c42fd ntdll!LdrGetProcedureAddressEx+0×2aa
00000000`00325950 00000000`774c1ddc ntdll!LdrpInitializeProcess+0×1a0b
00000000`00325958 00000000`774c1937 ntdll! ?? ::FNODOBFM::`string'+0×28ff0
00000000`00325960 00000000`774ac34e ntdll!LdrInitializeThunk+0xe
00000000`00325968 00000000`00000000
00000000`00325970 00000000`00000000
00000000`00325978 000a0008`00004801
00000000`00325980 00000000`7751998a ntdll! ?? ::FNODOBFM::`string'+0xdc1a
00000000`00325988 00000000`774bdaee ntdll!RtlCreateHeap+0×56e
00000000`00325990 00000000`774c47ff ntdll!CsrpConnectToServer+0×41f
00000000`00325998 00000000`774c43c5 ntdll!CsrClientConnectToServer+0×230
00000000`003259a0 000007fe`fd5ee232 KERNELBASE!KernelBaseDllInitialize+0×148
00000000`003259a8 00000000`774bb108 ntdll!LdrpRunInitializeRoutines+0×1fe
00000000`003259b0 00000000`774c42fd ntdll!LdrGetProcedureAddressEx+0×2aa
00000000`003259b8 00000000`774c1ddc ntdll!LdrpInitializeProcess+0×1a0b
00000000`003259c0 00000000`774c1937 ntdll! ?? ::FNODOBFM::`string'+0×28ff0
00000000`003259c8 00000000`774ac34e ntdll!LdrInitializeThunk+0xe
00000000`003259d0 00000000`00000000
00000000`003259d8 00080009`00003801
00000000`003259e0 000007fe`fd5edf81 KERNELBASE!NlsProcessInitialize+0×11
00000000`003259e8 000007fe`fd604439 KERNELBASE!BaseNlsDllInitialize+0×29
00000000`003259f0 000007fe`fd5ee446 KERNELBASE!KernelBaseDllInitialize+0×40c
00000000`003259f8 00000000`774bb108 ntdll!LdrpRunInitializeRoutines+0×1fe
00000000`00325a00 00000000`774c42fd ntdll!LdrGetProcedureAddressEx+0×2aa
00000000`00325a08 00000000`774c1ddc ntdll!LdrpInitializeProcess+0×1a0b
00000000`00325a10 00000000`774c1937 ntdll! ?? ::FNODOBFM::`string'+0×28ff0
00000000`00325a18 00000000`774ac34e ntdll!LdrInitializeThunk+0xe
00000000`00325a20 00000000`00000000
00000000`00325a28 0008000a`00003801
00000000`00325a30 000007fe`fd5edfa0 KERNELBASE!NlsProcessInitialize+0×30
00000000`00325a38 000007fe`fd604439 KERNELBASE!BaseNlsDllInitialize+0×29
00000000`00325a40 000007fe`fd5ee446 KERNELBASE!KernelBaseDllInitialize+0×40c
00000000`00325a48 00000000`774bb108 ntdll!LdrpRunInitializeRoutines+0×1fe
00000000`00325a50 00000000`774c42fd ntdll!LdrGetProcedureAddressEx+0×2aa
00000000`00325a58 00000000`774c1ddc ntdll!LdrpInitializeProcess+0×1a0b
00000000`00325a60 00000000`774c1937 ntdll! ?? ::FNODOBFM::`string'+0×28ff0
00000000`00325a68 00000000`774ac34e ntdll!LdrInitializeThunk+0xe
00000000`00325a70 00000000`00000000
00000000`00325a78 0007000b`00003801
00000000`00325a80 000007fe`fd604a21 KERNELBASE!BasepInitComputerNameCache+0×11
00000000`00325a88 000007fe`fd603d20 KERNELBASE!KernelBaseDllInitialize+0×419
00000000`00325a90 00000000`774bb108 ntdll!LdrpRunInitializeRoutines+0×1fe
00000000`00325a98 00000000`774c42fd ntdll!LdrGetProcedureAddressEx+0×2aa
00000000`00325aa0 00000000`774c1ddc ntdll!LdrpInitializeProcess+0×1a0b
00000000`00325aa8 00000000`774c1937 ntdll! ?? ::FNODOBFM::`string'+0×28ff0
00000000`00325ab0 00000000`774ac34e ntdll!LdrInitializeThunk+0xe
00000000`00325ab8 00000000`00000000
00000000`00325ac0 00000000`00000000
00000000`00325ac8 0006000c`00002801
00000000`00325ad0 00000000`77375699 kernel32!BaseDllInitialize+0×2f9
00000000`00325ad8 00000000`774bb108 ntdll!LdrpRunInitializeRoutines+0×1fe
00000000`00325ae0 00000000`774c42fd ntdll!LdrGetProcedureAddressEx+0×2aa
00000000`00325ae8 00000000`774c1ddc ntdll!LdrpInitializeProcess+0×1a0b
```

```
00000000`00325af0 00000000`774c1937 ntdll! ?? ::FNODOBFM::`string'+0x28ff0
00000000`00325af8 00000000`774ac34e ntdll!LdrInitializeThunk+0xe
00000000`00325b00 00000000`00000000
00000000`00325b08 0007000d`00003801
00000000`00325b10 00000000`773771f7
kernel32!InitializeConsoleConnectionInfo+0xe7
00000000`00325b18 00000000`773756ae kernel32!BaseDllInitialize+0x30e
00000000`00325b20 00000000`774bb108 ntdll!LdrpRunInitializeRoutines+0x1fe
00000000`00325b28 00000000`774c42fd ntdll!LdrGetProcedureAddressEx+0x2aa
00000000`00325b30 00000000`774c1ddc ntdll!LdrpInitializeProcess+0x1a0b
00000000`00325b38 00000000`774c1937 ntdll! ?? ::FNODOBFM::`string'+0x28ff0
00000000`00325b40 00000000`774ac34e ntdll!LdrInitializeThunk+0xe
00000000`00325b48 00000000`00000000
00000000`00325b50 00000000`00000000
00000000`00325b58 0009000e`00004801
00000000`00325b60 00000000`774bda86 ntdll!RtlCreateHeap+0x506
00000000`00325b68 00000000`773787f7 kernel32!ConsoleConnect+0x1d7
00000000`00325b70 00000000`773770de kernel32!ConnectConsoleInternal+0x147
00000000`00325b78 00000000`773756fe kernel32!BaseDllInitialize+0x35e
00000000`00325b80 00000000`774bb108 ntdll!LdrpRunInitializeRoutines+0x1fe
00000000`00325b88 00000000`774c42fd ntdll!LdrGetProcedureAddressEx+0x2aa
00000000`00325b90 00000000`774c1ddc ntdll!LdrpInitializeProcess+0x1a0b
00000000`00325b98 00000000`774c1937 ntdll! ?? ::FNODOBFM::`string'+0x28ff0
00000000`00325ba0 00000000`774ac34e ntdll!LdrInitializeThunk+0xe
00000000`00325ba8 00000000`00000000
00000000`00325bb0 00000000`00000000
00000000`00325bb8 000a000f`00004801
00000000`00325bc0 00000000`7751998a ntdll! ?? ::FNODOBFM::`string'+0xdc1a
00000000`00325bc8 00000000`774bdaee ntdll!RtlCreateHeap+0x56e
00000000`00325bd0 00000000`773787f7 kernel32!ConsoleConnect+0x1d7
00000000`00325bd8 00000000`773770de kernel32!ConnectConsoleInternal+0x147
00000000`00325be0 00000000`773756fe kernel32!BaseDllInitialize+0x35e
00000000`00325be8 00000000`774bb108 ntdll!LdrpRunInitializeRoutines+0x1fe
00000000`00325bf0 00000000`774c42fd ntdll!LdrGetProcedureAddressEx+0x2aa
00000000`00325bf8 00000000`774c1ddc ntdll!LdrpInitializeProcess+0x1a0b
00000000`00325c00 00000000`774c1937 ntdll! ?? ::FNODOBFM::`string'+0x28ff0
00000000`00325c08 00000000`774ac34e ntdll!LdrInitializeThunk+0xe
00000000`00325c10 00000000`00000000
00000000`00325c18 00060010`00002801
00000000`00325c20 00000000`773757dc kernel32!BaseDllInitialize+0x43c
00000000`00325c28 00000000`774bb108 ntdll!LdrpRunInitializeRoutines+0x1fe
00000000`00325c30 00000000`774c42fd ntdll!LdrGetProcedureAddressEx+0x2aa
00000000`00325c38 00000000`774c1ddc ntdll!LdrpInitializeProcess+0x1a0b
00000000`00325c40 00000000`774c1937 ntdll! ?? ::FNODOBFM::`string'+0x28ff0
00000000`00325c48 00000000`774ac34e ntdll!LdrInitializeThunk+0xe
00000000`00325c50 00000000`00000000
00000000`00325c58 00060011`00002801
00000000`00325c60 00000000`7737582c kernel32!BaseDllInitialize+0x48c
00000000`00325c68 00000000`774bb108 ntdll!LdrpRunInitializeRoutines+0x1fe
00000000`00325c70 00000000`774c42fd ntdll!LdrGetProcedureAddressEx+0x2aa
00000000`00325c78 00000000`774c1ddc ntdll!LdrpInitializeProcess+0x1a0b
00000000`00325c80 00000000`774c1937 ntdll! ?? ::FNODOBFM::`string'+0x28ff0
00000000`00325c88 00000000`774ac34e ntdll!LdrInitializeThunk+0xe
00000000`00325c90 00000000`00000000
00000000`00325c98 00060012`0000280e
00000000`00325ca0 000007fe`fd5e37aa
KERNELBASE!InitializeCriticalSectionAndSpinCount+0xa
00000000`00325ca8 00000001`3fd7319f AllocFree!_mtinitlocks+0x43
00000000`00325cb0 00000001`3fd717fc AllocFree!_mtinit+0x10
00000000`00325cb8 00000001`3fd710e4 AllocFree!__tmainCRTStartup+0x94
```

```
00000000`00325cc0 00000000`773759ed kernel32!BaseThreadInitThunk+0xd
00000000`00325cc8 00000000`774ac541 ntdll!RtlUserThreadStart+0x1d
00000000`00325cd0 00000000`00000000
00000000`00325cd8 000b0013`00005801
00000000`00325ce0 00000000`774c1131
ntdll!RtlpActivateLowFragmentationHeap+0x181
00000000`00325ce8 00000000`774c0f97 ntdll!RtlpPerformHeapMaintenance+0x27
00000000`00325cf0 00000000`774c0f5b ntdll!RtlpAllocateHeap+0x1819
00000000`00325cf8 00000000`774d34d8 ntdll!RtlAllocateHeap+0x16c
00000000`00325d00 00000000`774a9300
ntdll!RtlInitializeCriticalSectionAndSpinCount+0x183
00000000`00325d08 000007fe`fd5e37aa
KERNELBASE!InitializeCriticalSectionAndSpinCount+0xa
00000000`00325d10 00000001`3fd7319f AllocFree!_mtinitlocks+0x43
00000000`00325d18 00000001`3fd717fc AllocFree!_mtinit+0x10
00000000`00325d20 00000001`3fd710e4 AllocFree!__tmainCRTStartup+0x94
00000000`00325d28 00000000`773759ed kernel32!BaseThreadInitThunk+0xd
00000000`00325d30 00000000`774ac541 ntdll!RtlUserThreadStart+0x1d
00000000`00325d38 00000000`00000000
00000000`00325d40 00000000`00000000
00000000`00325d48 00070014`00003801
00000000`00325d50 000007fe`fd5e37aa
KERNELBASE!InitializeCriticalSectionAndSpinCount+0xa
00000000`00325d58 00000001`3fd7312f AllocFree!_mtinitlocknum+0x8f
00000000`00325d60 00000001`3fd72ff7 AllocFree!_lock+0x23
00000000`00325d68 00000001`3fd71f9b AllocFree!_ioinit+0x2f
00000000`00325d70 00000001`3fd71115 AllocFree!__tmainCRTStartup+0xc5
00000000`00325d78 00000000`773759ed kernel32!BaseThreadInitThunk+0xd
00000000`00325d80 00000000`774ac541 ntdll!RtlUserThreadStart+0x1d
00000000`00325d88 00000000`00000000
00000000`00325d90 00000000`00000000
00000000`00325d98 00050015`00002803
00000000`00325da0 000007fe`fd5e37aa
KERNELBASE!InitializeCriticalSectionAndSpinCount+0xa
00000000`00325da8 00000001`3fd72239 AllocFree!_ioinit+0x2cd
00000000`00325db0 00000001`3fd71115 AllocFree!__tmainCRTStartup+0xc5
00000000`00325db8 00000000`773759ed kernel32!BaseThreadInitThunk+0xd
00000000`00325dc0 00000000`774ac541 ntdll!RtlUserThreadStart+0x1d
00000000`00325dc8 00000000`00000000
00000000`00325dd0 00000000`00000000
[...]
```

This database corresponds to this simple program:

```
int _tmain(int argc, _TCHAR* argv[])
{
    free(malloc(256));
    Sleep(-1);
    return 0;
}
```

Wait Chain (Modules)

Most if not all **Wait Chain** (Volume 1, page 482) patterns are about waiting for some synchronization objects. **Stack Traces** (Volume 1, page 395) of involved threads may point to **Blocking** (Volume 6, page 54) and **Top** (Volume 6, page 62) modules. In some situations we may consider a module (which functions were called) itself as a pseudo-synchronization object where a module (who called it) is waiting for it to return back (to become "signaled"). All this is problem and context dependent where some intermediate modules may be **Pass Through** (Volume 3, page 129) or **Well-Tested** (Volume 6, page 48). When we see module inversion, such as in the case of callbacks we may provisionally suspect some kind of a deadlock and then investigate these threads in terms of synchronization objects or their corresponding source code:

TID 100

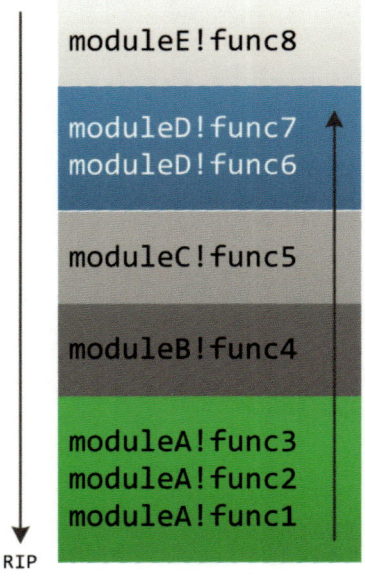

TID 200

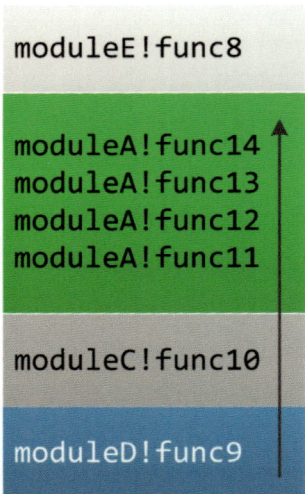

Insufficient Memory (Stack Trace Database)

Once we have seen a sequence of process memory dumps with the largest one almost 4GB. They were all saved from the process with growing memory consumption from 200MB initially. Initially, we suspected process heap **Memory Leak** (Volume 1, page 356). However, heap statistics (**!heap -s**) was normal. There were not even large block allocations (Volume 5, page 315). The dumps were also supplied with UMDH logs, but their difference only showed **Memory Fluctuation** (page 35) and not increase. **Stack Trace Collection** (Volume 1, page 409) revealed one **Spiking Thread** (Volume 1, page 305) was logging a heap allocation into the user mode stack trace database. We could also see that it was **Distributed Spike** (Volume 6, page 99). Inspection of address space showed a large number of sequential regions of the same size with **Stack Trace Database** (page 51) entries inside. So we concluded that it was stack trace logging **Instrumentation Side Effect** (Volume 6, page 77) and advised to limit stack backtrace size in *gflags.exe*.

To make sure we understood that problem correctly, we decided to model it. We did not come to the same results probably due to different logging implementation, but memory dumps clearly show the possibility of **Insufficient Memory** pattern variant. Here's the source code:

```
void foo20 (int size)
{
    free(malloc(size));
}

#define FOO(x,y) void foo##x (int size) { foo##y(size); }

FOO(19,20)
FOO(18,19)
FOO(17,18)
FOO(16,17)
FOO(15,16)
FOO(14,15)
FOO(13,14)
FOO(12,13)
FOO(11,12)
FOO(10,11)
FOO(9,10)
FOO(8,9)
FOO(7,8)
FOO(6,7)
FOO(5,6)
FOO(4,5)
```

```
FOO(3,4)
FOO(2,3)
FOO(1,2)

typedef void (*PFN) (int);

#define ARRSZ 20

PFN pfnArr[ARRSZ]  = {foo1, foo2, foo3, foo4, foo5, foo6, foo7,
    foo8, foo9, foo10, foo11, foo12, foo13, foo14,
    foo15, foo16, foo17, foo18, foo19, foo20};

int _tmain(int argc, _TCHAR* argv[])
{
    int i;
    for (i = 1; i < 1000000000; ++i)
    {
        pfnArr[i%ARRSZ](i);
    }
    Sleep(-1);
    return 0;
}
```

It allocates and then freezes heap entries of different size from 1 byte to 1,000,000,000 bytes all with different 20 possible stack traces. We choose different stack traces to increase the number of different *{size, stack backtrace}* pairs as the several allocations of a similar size having the same stack trace may be recorded only once in the database. We emulate different stack traces by calling different entries in *pfnArr*. Each call then leads to *foo20,* but the resulting stack trace depth is different. We also enabled *"Create user mode stack trace database"* checkbox in *gflags.exe* for our application called *AllocFree.exe*.

Then we see the expansion of **Stack Trace Database** regions (addresses are different because memory dumps were taken from different application runs):

```
0:000> !address
[...]
; Start         End          Size
+ 0`00240000 0`00312000 0`000d2000 MEM_PRIVATE MEM_COMMIT PAGE_READWRITE Other [Stack Trace
Database]
0`00312000 0`01a37000 0`01725000 MEM_PRIVATE MEM_RESERVE Other [Stack Trace Database]
0`01a37000 0`01a40000 0`00009000 MEM_PRIVATE MEM_COMMIT PAGE_READWRITE Other [Stack Trace
Database]

0:000> !address
[...]
+ 0`001b0000 0`0188c000 0`016dc000 MEM_PRIVATE MEM_COMMIT PAGE_READWRITE Other [Stack Trace
Database]
0`0188c000 0`0188d000 0`00001000 MEM_PRIVATE MEM_RESERVE Other [Stack Trace Database]
0`0188d000 0`019b0000 0`00123000 MEM_PRIVATE MEM_COMMIT PAGE_READWRITE Other [Stack Trace
Database]
```

Heap stays the same:

```
0:000> !heap -s
NtGlobalFlag enables following debugging aids for new heaps:
stack back traces
LFH Key                 : 0x000000f841c4f9c0
Termination on corruption : ENABLED
          Heap     Flags   Reserv  Commit  Virt   Free  List   UCR  Virt  Lock
  Fast
                            (k)     (k)     (k)    (k) length       blocks
cont.
 heap
-------------------------------------------------------------------------------
------
0000000001a40000 08000002    4096    1444    4096   1164    4     3    0     0
    LFH
External fragmentation  80 % (4 free blocks)
0000000000010000 08008000      64       4      64      1    1     1    0     0
0000000000020000 08008000      64      64      64     61    1     1    0     0
-------------------------------------------------------------------------------
------

0:000> !heap -s
NtGlobalFlag enables following debugging aids for new heaps:
stack back traces
LFH Key                 : 0x000000473a639107
Termination on corruption : ENABLED
          Heap     Flags   Reserv  Commit  Virt   Free  List   UCR  Virt  Lock
  Fast
                            (k)     (k)     (k)    (k) length       blocks
cont.
 heap
-------------------------------------------------------------------------------
------
00000000019c0000 08000002    4096    1444    4096   1164    4     3    0     0
    LFH
External fragmentation  80 % (4 free blocks)
0000000000010000 08008000      64       4      64      1    1     1    0     0
0000000000020000 08008000      64      64      64     61    1     1    0     0
-------------------------------------------------------------------------------
------
```

However, we see the thread consuming much CPU and that it was caught while logging stack backtrace:

```
0:000> kc
Call Site
ntdll!RtlpStdLogCapturedStackTrace
ntdll!RtlStdLogStackTrace
ntdll!RtlLogStackBackTraceEx
ntdll!RtlpAllocateHeap
ntdll!RtlAllocateHeap
AllocFree!_heap_alloc
AllocFree!malloc
AllocFree!foo20
AllocFree!foo19
AllocFree!foo18
AllocFree!foo17
AllocFree!foo16
AllocFree!foo15
AllocFree!foo14
AllocFree!foo13
AllocFree!foo12
AllocFree!foo11
AllocFree!foo10
AllocFree!foo9
AllocFree!foo8
AllocFree!foo7
AllocFree!foo6
AllocFree!foo5
AllocFree!foo4
AllocFree!foo3
AllocFree!foo2
AllocFree!foo1
AllocFree!wmain
AllocFree!__tmainCRTStartup
kernel32!BaseThreadInitThunk
ntdll!RtlUserThreadStart

0:000> !runaway f
 User Mode Time
  Thread       Time
   0:53b8        0 days 3:22:02.354
 Kernel Mode Time
  Thread       Time
   0:53b8        0 days 0:20:39.022
 Elapsed Time
  Thread       Time
   0:53b8        0 days 10:11:23.596
```

If we dump some portion of the region we see recorded stack backtraces:

```
0:000> dps 0`0188c000-200 L200/8
00000000`0188be00 00000000`77891142 ntdll!RtlpAllocateHeap+0x33bd
00000000`0188be08 00000000`778834d8 ntdll!RtlAllocateHeap+0x16c
00000000`0188be10 00000001`3fcc13cb AllocFree!malloc+0x5b
00000000`0188be18 00000001`3fcc1015 AllocFree!foo20+0x15
00000000`0188be20 00000001`3fcc1041 AllocFree!foo19+0x11
00000000`0188be28 00000001`3fcc1061 AllocFree!foo18+0x11
00000000`0188be30 00000001`3fcc12e3 AllocFree!wmain+0x53
00000000`0188be38 00000001`3fcc156c AllocFree!__tmainCRTStartup+0x144
00000000`0188be40 00000000`777259ed kernel32!BaseThreadInitThunk+0xd
00000000`0188be48 00000000`7785c541 ntdll!RtlUserThreadStart+0x1d
00000000`0188be50 00000000`0188b1d0
00000000`0188be58 0009457d`00024fff
00000000`0188be60 00000000`77891142 ntdll!RtlpAllocateHeap+0x33bd
00000000`0188be68 00000000`778834d8 ntdll!RtlAllocateHeap+0x16c
00000000`0188be70 00000001`3fcc13cb AllocFree!malloc+0x5b
00000000`0188be78 00000001`3fcc1015 AllocFree!foo20+0x15
00000000`0188be80 00000001`3fcc1041 AllocFree!foo19+0x11
00000000`0188be88 00000001`3fcc12e3 AllocFree!wmain+0x53
00000000`0188be90 00000001`3fcc156c AllocFree!__tmainCRTStartup+0x144
00000000`0188be98 00000000`777259ed kernel32!BaseThreadInitThunk+0xd
00000000`0188bea0 00000000`7785c541 ntdll!RtlUserThreadStart+0x1d
00000000`0188bea8 00000000`00000000
00000000`0188beb0 00000000`0188b230
00000000`0188beb8 0008457e`00023fff
00000000`0188bec0 00000000`77891142 ntdll!RtlpAllocateHeap+0x33bd
00000000`0188bec8 00000000`778834d8 ntdll!RtlAllocateHeap+0x16c
00000000`0188bed0 00000001`3fcc13cb AllocFree!malloc+0x5b
00000000`0188bed8 00000001`3fcc1015 AllocFree!foo20+0x15
00000000`0188bee0 00000001`3fcc12e3 AllocFree!wmain+0x53
00000000`0188bee8 00000001`3fcc156c AllocFree!__tmainCRTStartup+0x144
00000000`0188bef0 00000000`777259ed kernel32!BaseThreadInitThunk+0xd
00000000`0188bef8 00000000`7785c541 ntdll!RtlUserThreadStart+0x1d
00000000`0188bf00 00000000`0188b280
00000000`0188bf08 001b457f`0002dfff
00000000`0188bf10 00000000`77891142 ntdll!RtlpAllocateHeap+0x33bd
00000000`0188bf18 00000000`778834d8 ntdll!RtlAllocateHeap+0x16c
00000000`0188bf20 00000001`3fcc13cb AllocFree!malloc+0x5b
00000000`0188bf28 00000001`3fcc1015 AllocFree!foo20+0x15
00000000`0188bf30 00000001`3fcc1041 AllocFree!foo19+0x11
00000000`0188bf38 00000001`3fcc1061 AllocFree!foo18+0x11
00000000`0188bf40 00000001`3fcc1081 AllocFree!foo17+0x11
00000000`0188bf48 00000001`3fcc10a1 AllocFree!foo16+0x11
00000000`0188bf50 00000001`3fcc10c1 AllocFree!foo15+0x11
00000000`0188bf58 00000001`3fcc10e1 AllocFree!foo14+0x11
00000000`0188bf60 00000001`3fcc1101 AllocFree!foo13+0x11
00000000`0188bf68 00000001`3fcc1121 AllocFree!foo12+0x11
00000000`0188bf70 00000001`3fcc1141 AllocFree!foo11+0x11
00000000`0188bf78 00000001`3fcc1161 AllocFree!foo10+0x11
```

```
00000000`0188bf80 00000001`3fcc1181 AllocFree!foo9+0x11
00000000`0188bf88 00000001`3fcc11a1 AllocFree!foo8+0x11
00000000`0188bf90 00000001`3fcc11c1 AllocFree!foo7+0x11
00000000`0188bf98 00000001`3fcc11e1 AllocFree!foo6+0x11
00000000`0188bfa0 00000001`3fcc1201 AllocFree!foo5+0x11
00000000`0188bfa8 00000001`3fcc1221 AllocFree!foo4+0x11
00000000`0188bfb0 00000001`3fcc1241 AllocFree!foo3+0x11
00000000`0188bfb8 00000001`3fcc1261 AllocFree!foo2+0x11
00000000`0188bfc0 00000001`3fcc1281 AllocFree!foo1+0x11
00000000`0188bfc8 00000001`3fcc12e3 AllocFree!wmain+0x53
00000000`0188bfd0 00000001`3fcc156c AllocFree!__tmainCRTStartup+0x144
00000000`0188bfd8 00000000`777259ed kernel32!BaseThreadInitThunk+0xd
00000000`0188bfe0 00000000`7785c541 ntdll!RtlUserThreadStart+0x1d
00000000`0188bfe8 00000000`00000000
00000000`0188bff0 00000000`00000000
00000000`0188bff8 00000000`00000000
```

Insufficient Memory (Region)

While working on **Insufficient Memory** pattern for stack trace database (page 57) we noticed the expansion of certain memory regions. Of course, after some time expanding region consumes remaining free or reserved space available before some other region. Generalizing from this, we may say there can be **Insufficient Memory** pattern variant for any expanding region. Region expansion may also be implemented via its move into some other position in memory virtual address space. This movement also has its limits. For example, we created this modeling application and found out it stops reallocating memory long before it reaches 2,000,000,000-byte size:

```
int _tmain(int argc, _TCHAR* argv[])
{
        int i = 100000000;
        void *p = malloc(i);
        for (i = 200000000; i < 2000000000; i+=100000000)
        {
                p = realloc(p, i);
                getc(stdin);
        }
        return 0;
}
```

We took memory dumps after each loop iteration and after 6 or 8 iterations the memory size was constant, and there were no further reallocations:

```
0:000> !heap -s
[...]
Virtual block: 0000000006370000 - 0000000006370000 (size 0000000000000000)
[...]

0:000> !address
[...]
; Start        End          Size
+ 0`00550000 0`06370000 0`05e20000 MEM_FREE PAGE_NOACCESS Free
+ 0`06370000 0`1222d000 0`0bebd000 MEM_PRIVATE MEM_COMMIT PAGE_READWRITE Heap [ID: 0;
Handle: 0000000000310000; Type: Large block]
+ 0`1222d000 0`77710000 0`654e3000 MEM_FREE PAGE_NOACCESS Free
+ 0`77710000 0`77711000 0`00001000 MEM_IMAGE MEM_COMMIT PAGE_READONLY Image [kernel32;
"C:\windows\system32\kernel32.dll"]
[...]

0:000> !heap -s
[...]
Virtual block: 0000000012230000 - 0000000012230000 (size 0000000000000000)
[...]
```

```
0:000> !address
[...]
+ 0`005d0000 0`12230000 0`11c60000 MEM_FREE PAGE_NOACCESS Free
+ 0`12230000 0`2404b000 0`11e1b000 MEM_PRIVATE MEM_COMMIT PAGE_READWRITE Heap [ID: 0;
Handle: 0000000000310000; Type: Large block]
+ 0`2404b000 0`77710000 0`536c5000 MEM_FREE PAGE_NOACCESS Free
+ 0`77710000 0`77711000 0`00001000 MEM_IMAGE MEM_COMMIT PAGE_READONLY Image [kernel32;
"C:\windows\system32\kernel32.dll"]
[...]

0:000> !heap -s
[...]
Virtual block: 0000000024050000 - 0000000024050000 (size 0000000000000000)
[...]

0:000> !address
[...]
+ 0`00590000 0`24050000 0`23ac0000 MEM_FREE PAGE_NOACCESS Free
+ 0`24050000 0`3bdc9000 0`17d79000 MEM_PRIVATE MEM_COMMIT PAGE_READWRITE Heap [ID: 0;
Handle: 0000000000310000; Type: Large block]
+ 0`3bdc9000 0`77710000 0`3b947000 MEM_FREE PAGE_NOACCESS Free
+ 0`77710000 0`77711000 0`00001000 MEM_IMAGE MEM_COMMIT PAGE_READONLY Image [kernel32;
"C:\windows\system32\kernel32.dll"]
[...]
```

We skip a few iterations and finally come to a region that does not move and not increase:

```
0:000> !heap -s
[...]
Virtual block: 0000000041d30000 - 0000000041d30000 (size 0000000000000000)
[...]


0:000> !address
[...]
+ 0`006c0000 0`41d30000 0`41670000 MEM_FREE PAGE_NOACCESS Free
+ 0`41d30000 0`6b8c3000 0`29b93000 MEM_PRIVATE MEM_COMMIT PAGE_READWRITE Heap [ID: 0;
Handle: 0000000000310000; Type: Large block]
+ 0`6b8c3000 0`77710000 0`0be4d000 MEM_FREE PAGE_NOACCESS Free
+ 0`77710000 0`77711000 0`00001000 MEM_IMAGE MEM_COMMIT PAGE_READONLY Image [kernel32;
"C:\windows\system32\kernel32.dll"]
[...]
```

Memory Leak (Regions)

The set of memory dumps that prompted to introduce **Insufficient Memory** pattern for stack trace database (page 57) also prompted to include a variant of **Memory Leak** pattern related to regions of virtual memory address space. We created this simple modeling application:

```
int _tmain(int argc, _TCHAR* argv[])
{
      int i,j;
      for (i = 1; i < 1000; ++i)
      {
            for (j = 1; j < 1000; ++j)
            {
                  VirtualAlloc(NULL, 0x10000, MEM_RESERVE,
                              PAGE_EXECUTE_READWRITE);
            }
            getc(stdin);
      }
      return 0;
}
```

We allocated only reserved memory regions. Committing them would probably at some stage manifest **Insufficient Memory** patterns for committed memory (Volume 1, page 302) and physical memory (Volume 3, page 104). So we took a few consecutive memory dumps and saw the ever increasing number of regions allocated at greater and greater virtual addresses:

```
0:000> !address
[...]
*        0`04070000        0`04080000        0`00010000 MEM_PRIVATE
MEM_RESERVE                                  <unclassified>
*        0`04080000        0`04090000        0`00010000 MEM_PRIVATE
MEM_RESERVE                                  <unclassified>
*        0`04090000        0`040a0000        0`00010000 MEM_PRIVATE
MEM_RESERVE                                  <unclassified>
*        0`040a0000        0`040b0000        0`00010000 MEM_PRIVATE
MEM_RESERVE                                  <unclassified>
*        0`040b0000        0`040c0000        0`00010000 MEM_PRIVATE
MEM_RESERVE                                  <unclassified>
*        0`040c0000        0`040d0000        0`00010000 MEM_PRIVATE
MEM_RESERVE                                  <unclassified>
*        0`040d0000        0`040e0000        0`00010000 MEM_PRIVATE
MEM_RESERVE                                  <unclassified>
*        0`040e0000        0`040f0000        0`00010000 MEM_PRIVATE
MEM_RESERVE                                  <unclassified>
*        0`040f0000        0`04100000        0`00010000 MEM_PRIVATE
MEM_RESERVE                                  <unclassified>
*        0`04100000        0`04110000        0`00010000 MEM_PRIVATE
MEM_RESERVE                                  <unclassified>
*        0`04110000        0`04120000        0`00010000 MEM_PRIVATE
MEM_RESERVE                                  <unclassified>
*        0`04120000        0`04130000        0`00010000 MEM_PRIVATE
```

```
MEM_RESERVE                                    <unclassified>
*        0`04130000      0`04140000      0`00010000 MEM_PRIVATE
MEM_RESERVE                                    <unclassified>
*        0`04140000      0`04260000      0`00120000              MEM_FREE    PAGE_NOACCES
S                        Free
[...]


0:000> !address
[...]
*        0`2eec0000      0`2eed0000      0`00010000 MEM_PRIVATE
MEM_RESERVE                                    <unclassified>
*        0`2eed0000      0`2eee0000      0`00010000 MEM_PRIVATE
MEM_RESERVE                                    <unclassified>
*        0`2eee0000      0`2eef0000      0`00010000 MEM_PRIVATE
MEM_RESERVE                                    <unclassified>
*        0`2eef0000      0`2ef00000      0`00010000 MEM_PRIVATE
MEM_RESERVE                                    <unclassified>
*        0`2ef00000      0`2ef10000      0`00010000 MEM_PRIVATE
MEM_RESERVE                                    <unclassified>
*        0`2ef10000      0`2ef20000      0`00010000 MEM_PRIVATE
MEM_RESERVE                                    <unclassified>
*        0`2ef20000      0`2ef30000      0`00010000 MEM_PRIVATE
MEM_RESERVE                                    <unclassified>
*        0`2ef30000      0`2ef40000      0`00010000 MEM_PRIVATE
MEM_RESERVE                                    <unclassified>
*        0`2ef40000      0`2ef50000      0`00010000 MEM_PRIVATE
MEM_RESERVE                                    <unclassified>
*        0`2ef50000      0`2ef60000      0`00010000 MEM_PRIVATE
MEM_RESERVE                                    <unclassified>
*        0`2ef60000      0`2ef70000      0`00010000 MEM_PRIVATE
MEM_RESERVE                                    <unclassified>
*        0`2ef70000      0`2ef80000      0`00010000 MEM_PRIVATE
MEM_RESERVE                                    <unclassified>
*        0`2ef80000      0`2ef90000      0`00010000 MEM_PRIVATE
MEM_RESERVE                                    <unclassified>
*        0`2ef90000      0`2efa0000      0`00010000 MEM_PRIVATE
MEM_RESERVE                                    <unclassified>
*        0`2efa0000      0`2efb0000      0`00010000 MEM_PRIVATE
MEM_RESERVE                                    <unclassified>
*        0`2efb0000      0`2efc0000      0`00010000 MEM_PRIVATE
MEM_RESERVE                                    <unclassified>
*        0`2efc0000      0`2efd0000      0`00010000 MEM_PRIVATE
MEM_RESERVE                                    <unclassified>
*        0`2efd0000      0`2efe0000      0`00010000 MEM_PRIVATE
MEM_RESERVE                                    <unclassified>
*        0`2efe0000      0`2eff0000      0`00010000 MEM_PRIVATE
MEM_RESERVE                                    <unclassified>
*        0`2eff0000      0`2f000000      0`00010000 MEM_PRIVATE
MEM_RESERVE                                    <unclassified>
*        0`2f000000      0`2f010000      0`00010000 MEM_PRIVATE
MEM_RESERVE                                    <unclassified>
*        0`2f010000      0`2f170000      0`00160000              MEM_FREE    PAGE_NOACCES
S                        Free
[...]
```

```
0:000> !address
[...]
*          0`697f0000        0`69800000        0`00010000 MEM_PRIVATE
MEM_RESERVE                                    <unclassified>
*          0`69800000        0`69810000        0`00010000 MEM_PRIVATE
MEM_RESERVE                                    <unclassified>
*          0`69810000        0`69820000        0`00010000 MEM_PRIVATE
MEM_RESERVE                                    <unclassified>
*          0`69820000        0`69830000        0`00010000 MEM_PRIVATE
MEM_RESERVE                                    <unclassified>
*          0`69830000        0`69840000        0`00010000 MEM_PRIVATE
MEM_RESERVE                                    <unclassified>
*          0`69840000        0`69850000        0`00010000 MEM_PRIVATE
MEM_RESERVE                                    <unclassified>
*          0`69850000        0`69860000        0`00010000 MEM_PRIVATE
MEM_RESERVE                                    <unclassified>
*          0`69860000        0`69870000        0`00010000 MEM_PRIVATE
MEM_RESERVE                                    <unclassified>
*          0`69870000        0`69880000        0`00010000 MEM_PRIVATE
MEM_RESERVE                                    <unclassified>
*          0`69880000        0`69890000        0`00010000 MEM_PRIVATE
MEM_RESERVE                                    <unclassified>
*          0`69890000        0`698a0000        0`00010000 MEM_PRIVATE
MEM_RESERVE                                    <unclassified>
*          0`698a0000        0`699e0000        0`00140000              MEM_FREE    PAGE_NOACCES
S                          Free
[...]


0:000> !address
[...]
*          0`c08c0000        0`c08d0000        0`00010000 MEM_PRIVATE
MEM_RESERVE                                    <unclassified>
*          0`c08d0000        0`c08e0000        0`00010000 MEM_PRIVATE
MEM_RESERVE                                    <unclassified>
*          0`c08e0000        0`c08f0000        0`00010000 MEM_PRIVATE
MEM_RESERVE                                    <unclassified>
*          0`c08f0000        0`c0900000        0`00010000 MEM_PRIVATE
MEM_RESERVE                                    <unclassified>
*          0`c0900000        0`c0910000        0`00010000 MEM_PRIVATE
MEM_RESERVE                                    <unclassified>
*          0`c0910000        0`c0920000        0`00010000 MEM_PRIVATE
MEM_RESERVE                                    <unclassified>
*          0`c0920000        0`c0930000        0`00010000 MEM_PRIVATE
MEM_RESERVE                                    <unclassified>
*          0`c0930000        0`c0960000        0`00030000              MEM_FREE    PAGE_NOACCES
S                          Free
[...]


0:000> !address
[...]
*          1`3d6a0000        1`3d6b0000        0`00010000 MEM_PRIVATE
MEM_RESERVE                                    <unclassified>
*          1`3d6b0000        1`3d6c0000        0`00010000 MEM_PRIVATE
MEM_RESERVE                                    <unclassified>
*          1`3d6c0000        1`3d6d0000        0`00010000 MEM_PRIVATE
MEM_RESERVE                                    <unclassified>
*          1`3d6d0000        1`3d6e0000        0`00010000 MEM_PRIVATE
MEM_RESERVE                                    <unclassified>
*          1`3d6e0000        1`3d6f0000        0`00010000 MEM_PRIVATE
MEM_RESERVE                                    <unclassified>
*          1`3d6f0000        1`3d700000        0`00010000 MEM_PRIVATE
MEM_RESERVE                                    <unclassified>
*          1`3d700000        1`3d710000        0`00010000 MEM_PRIVATE
MEM_RESERVE                                    <unclassified>
*          1`3d710000        1`3d720000        0`00010000 MEM_PRIVATE
MEM_RESERVE                                    <unclassified>
*          1`3d720000        1`3d730000        0`00010000 MEM_PRIVATE
MEM_RESERVE                                    <unclassified>
```

```
*       1`3d730000      1`3d7a0000      0`00070000          MEM_FREE    PAGE_NOACCES
S                     Free
[...]


0:000> !address -summary


--- Usage Summary --------------- RgnCount ------ Total Size --- %ofBusy %ofTotal
Free                                    15      7fe`c275e000 (    7.995 Tb)          99.94%
<unclassified>                       80928      1`3d193000 (    4.955 Gb)  99.86%    0.06%
Image                                   28      0`0034b000 (    3.293 Mb)   0.06%    0.00%
Stack                                    6      0`00200000 (    2.000 Mb)   0.04%    0.00%
MemoryMappedFile                         8      0`001af000 (    1.684 Mb)   0.03%    0.00%
TEB                                      2      0`00004000 (   16.000 kb)   0.00%    0.00%
PEB                                      1      0`00001000 (    4.000 kb)   0.00%    0.00%


--- Type Summary (for busy) ------ RgnCount ----------- Total Size -------- %ofBusy %ofTotal
MEM_PRIVATE                          80936      1`3d397000 (    4.957 Gb)  99.90%    0.06%
MEM_IMAGE                               29      0`0034c000 (    3.297 Mb)   0.06%    0.00%
MEM_MAPPED                               8      0`001af000 (    1.684 Mb)   0.03%    0.00%


--- State Summary --------------- RgnCount ----------- Total Size -------- %ofBusy %ofTotal
MEM_FREE                                15      7fe`c275e000 (    7.995 Tb)          99.94%
MEM_RESERVE                          80926      1`3d438000 (    4.957 Gb)  99.91%    0.06%
MEM_COMMIT                              47      0`0045a000 (    4.352 Mb)   0.09%    0.00%


--- Protect Summary (for commit) - RgnCount ----------- Total Size -------- %ofBusy %ofTotal
PAGE_EXECUTE_READ                        4      0`001ef000 (    1.934 Mb)   0.04%    0.00%
PAGE_READONLY                           19      0`001de000 (    1.867 Mb)   0.04%    0.00%
PAGE_READWRITE                          17      0`00080000 (  512.000 kb)   0.01%    0.00%
PAGE_WRITECOPY                           5      0`00008000 (   32.000 kb)   0.00%    0.00%
PAGE_READWRITE|PAGE_GUARD                2      0`00005000 (   20.000 kb)   0.00%    0.00%


--- Largest Region by Usage ----------- Base Address -------- Region Size ----------
Free                                         1`3fac7000      7fd`bdc79000 (    7.991 Tb)
<unclassified>                               0`7f0e0000      0`00f00000 (   15.000 Mb)
Image                                        0`77831000      0`00102000 (    1.008 Mb)
Stack                                        0`00170000      0`000fb000 (1004.000 kb)
MemoryMappedFile                             0`7efe5000      0`000fb000 (1004.000 kb)
TEB                                        7ff`fffdc000      0`00002000 (    8.000 kb)
PEB                                        7ff`fffd3000      0`00001000 (    4.000 kb)
```

Examination of such regions for **Execution Residue** (Volume 2, page 239) such as **Module Hint** (Volume 6, page 92) may point into further troubleshooting directions especially if live debugging is not possible.

Invalid Handle (Managed Space)

We recently encountered **Invalid Handle** (Volume 2, page 269) pattern in the context of .NET program execution. We decided to model it and wrote a small C# program:

```
namespace SafeHandle
{
    class Program
    {
        static void Main(string[] args)
        {
            SafeFileHandle hFile =
                new SafeFileHandle(new IntPtr(0xDEAD), true);
            Console.WriteLine("About to close");
            Console.ReadKey();
        }
    }
}
```

Of course, when we execute it nothing happens. Invalid handles are ignored by default. However, to change the behavior we enabled "*Enable close exception*" in *glags.exe*:

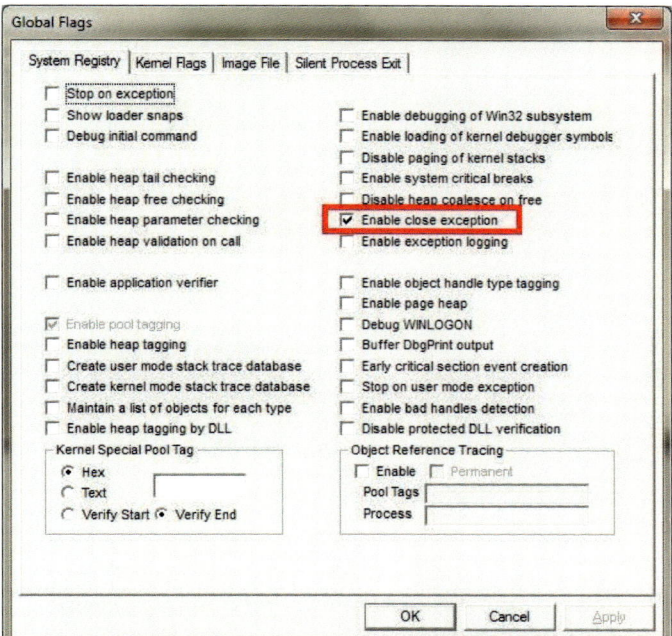

Moreover, if we run it we get this **Managed Stack Trace** (Volume 6, page 115):

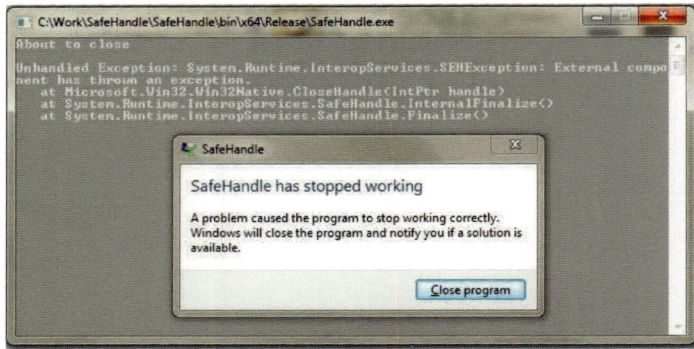

We could have detected invalid handle if we enabled *Application Verifier,* but then we would not have **Managed Code Exception** (Volume 1, page 331).

So we load a crash dump (saved because we enabled LocalDumps[10]) and load SOS extension:

```
0:002> lmv m clr
start end module name
000007fe`ed880000 000007fe`ee1eb000 clr (pdb symbols)
Loaded symbol image file: clr.dll
Image path: C:\Windows\Microsoft.NET\Framework64\v4.0.30319\clr.dll
[...]


0:002> .load C:\Windows\Microsoft.NET\Framework64\v4.0.30319\sos


0:002> !pe
Exception object: 0000000002ab5fe8
Exception type: System.Runtime.InteropServices.SEHException
Message: External component has thrown an exception.
InnerException:
StackTrace (generated):
SP IP Function
000000001B40EDD0 0000000000000000
mscorlib_ni!Microsoft.Win32.Win32Native.CloseHandle(IntPtr)+0×1
000000001B40F2F0 0000000000000000
mscorlib_ni!System.Runtime.InteropServices.SafeHandle.InternalFinalize()+0×1
000000001B40F2F0 000007FEEC62F7A6
mscorlib_ni!System.Runtime.InteropServices.SafeHandle.Finalize()+0×26
```

---

[10] http://msdn.microsoft.com/en-us/library/bb787181.aspx

```
StackTraceString:
HResult: 80004005
```

Our unmanaged **CLR Thread** (Volume 4, page 163) **Exception Stack Trace** (Volume 5, page 93) is quite simple:

```
0:002> k
Child-SP RetAddr Call Site
00000000`1b40d6e8 000007fe`fd651430 ntdll!NtWaitForMultipleObjects+0xa
00000000`1b40d6f0 00000000`77621723 KERNELBASE!WaitForMultipleObjectsEx+0xe8
00000000`1b40d7f0 00000000`7769b5e5
kernel32!WaitForMultipleObjectsExImplementation+0xb3
00000000`1b40d880 00000000`7769b767 kernel32!WerpReportFaultInternal+0x215
00000000`1b40d920 00000000`7769b7bf kernel32!WerpReportFault+0x77
00000000`1b40d950 00000000`7769b9dc kernel32!BasepReportFault+0x1f
00000000`1b40d980 00000000`778b3398 kernel32!UnhandledExceptionFilter+0x1fc
00000000`1b40da60 00000000`778385c8 ntdll! ?? ::FNODOBFM::`string'+0x2365
00000000`1b40da90 00000000`77849d2d ntdll!_C_specific_handler+0x8c
00000000`1b40db00 00000000`778391cf ntdll!RtlpExecuteHandlerForException+0xd
00000000`1b40db30 00000000`778397c8 ntdll!RtlDispatchException+0x45a
00000000`1b40e210 00000000`778712c7 ntdll!RtlRaiseException+0x22f
00000000`1b40ebc0 000007fe`fd651873 ntdll!KiRaiseUserExceptionDispatcher+0x3a
00000000`1b40ec90 00000000`77621991 KERNELBASE!CloseHandle+0x13
00000000`1b40ecc0 000007fe`ec720418 kernel32!CloseHandleImplementation+0x3d
00000000`1b40edd0 000007fe`ed8e9e03 mscorlib_ni+0x580418
00000000`1b40eea0 000007fe`ed8e9e7e clr!CallDescrWorkerInternal+0x83
00000000`1b40eee0 000007fe`ed8ec860 clr!CallDescrWorkerWithHandler+0x4a
00000000`1b40ef20 000007fe`ed8f1a1d clr!DispatchCallSimple+0x85
00000000`1b40efb0 000007fe`ed8f19ac clr!SafeHandle::RunReleaseMethod+0x69
00000000`1b40f050 000007fe`ed8f180a clr!SafeHandle::Release+0x122
00000000`1b40f120 000007fe`eda4863e clr!SafeHandle::Dispose+0x36
00000000`1b40f190 000007fe`ec62f7a6 clr!SafeHandle::Finalize+0xa2
00000000`1b40f2f0 000007fe`ed8e9d56 mscorlib_ni+0x48f7a6
00000000`1b40f330 000007fe`eda83c4e clr!FastCallFinalizeWorker+0x6
00000000`1b40f360 000007fe`eda83bc3 clr!MethodDesc::RequiresFullSlotNumber+0x72
00000000`1b40f3a0 000007fe`eda83b0f clr!MethodTable::CallFinalizer+0xa3
00000000`1b40f3e0 000007fe`ed9fee46 clr!SVR::CallFinalizer+0x5f
00000000`1b40f420 000007fe`ed9aac5b clr!SVR::CallFinalizer+0x102
00000000`1b40f4e0 000007fe`ed8f458c clr!WKS::GCHeap::IsPromoted+0xee
00000000`1b40f520 000007fe`ed8f451a clr!Frame::Pop+0x50
00000000`1b40f560 000007fe`ed8f4491
clr!COMCustomAttribute::PopSecurityContextFrame+0x192
00000000`1b40f660 000007fe`ed9d1bfe
clr!COMCustomAttribute::PopSecurityContextFrame+0xbd
00000000`1b40f6f0 000007fe`ed9d1e59 clr!ManagedThreadBase_NoADTransition+0x3f
00000000`1b40f750 000007fe`ed9533de clr!WKS::GCHeap::FinalizerThreadStart+0x193
00000000`1b40f790 00000000`776159ed clr!Thread::intermediateThreadProc+0x7d
00000000`1b40f850 00000000`7784c541 kernel32!BaseThreadInitThunk+0xd
00000000`1b40f880 00000000`00000000 ntdll!RtlUserThreadStart+0x1d
```

We see that exception processing happened during object finalization. We can infer the value of the handle (may be **Small Value**, Volume 7, page 191) via disassembly if this is possible:

```
0:002> kn
# Child-SP RetAddr Call Site
00 00000000`1b40d6e8 000007fe`fd651430 ntdll!NtWaitForMultipleObjects+0xa
01 00000000`1b40d6f0 000007fe`77621723 KERNELBASE!WaitForMultipleObjectsEx+0xe8
02 00000000`1b40d7f0 00000000`7769b5e5 kernel32!WaitForMultipleObjectsExImplementation+0xb3
03 00000000`1b40d880 00000000`7769b767 kernel32!WerpReportFaultInternal+0x215
04 00000000`1b40d920 00000000`7769b7bf kernel32!WerpReportFault+0x77
05 00000000`1b40d950 00000000`7769b9dc kernel32!BasepReportFault+0x1f
06 00000000`1b40d980 00000000`778b3398 kernel32!UnhandledExceptionFilter+0x1fc
07 00000000`1b40da60 00000000`778385c8 ntdll! ?? ::FNODOBFM::`string'+0x2365
08 00000000`1b40da90 00000000`77849d2d ntdll!_C_specific_handler+0x8c
09 00000000`1b40db00 00000000`778391cf ntdll!RtlpExecuteHandlerForException+0xd
0a 00000000`1b40db30 00000000`778397c8 ntdll!RtlDispatchException+0x45a
0b 00000000`1b40e210 00000000`778712c7 ntdll!RtlRaiseException+0x22f
0c 00000000`1b40ebc0 000007fe`fd651873 ntdll!KiRaiseUserExceptionDispatcher+0x3a
0d 00000000`1b40ec90 00000000`77621991 KERNELBASE!CloseHandle+0x13
0e 00000000`1b40ecc0 000007fe`ec720418 kernel32!CloseHandleImplementation+0x3d
0f 00000000`1b40edd0 000007fe`ed8e9e03 mscorlib_ni+0x580418
10 00000000`1b40eea0 000007fe`ed8e9e7e clr!CallDescrWorkerInternal+0x83
11 00000000`1b40eee0 000007fe`ed8ec860 clr!CallDescrWorkerWithHandler+0x4a
12 00000000`1b40ef20 000007fe`ed8f1a1d clr!DispatchCallSimple+0x85
13 00000000`1b40efb0 000007fe`ed8f19ac clr!SafeHandle::RunReleaseMethod+0x69
14 00000000`1b40f050 000007fe`ed8f180a clr!SafeHandle::Release+0x122
15 00000000`1b40f120 000007fe`eda4863e clr!SafeHandle::Dispose+0x36
16 00000000`1b40f190 000007fe`ec62f7a6 clr!SafeHandle::Finalize+0xa2
17 00000000`1b40f2f0 000007fe`ed8e9d56 mscorlib_ni+0x48f7a6
18 00000000`1b40f330 000007fe`eda83c4e clr!FastCallFinalizeWorker+0x6
19 00000000`1b40f360 000007fe`eda83bc3 clr!MethodDesc::RequiresFullSlotNumber+0x72
1a 00000000`1b40f3a0 000007fe`ed8a83b0f clr!MethodTable::CallFinalizer+0xa3
1b 00000000`1b40f3e0 000007fe`ed9fee46 clr!SVR::CallFinalizer+0x5f
1c 00000000`1b40f420 000007fe`ed9aac5b clr!SVR::CallFinalizer+0x102
1d 00000000`1b40f4e0 000007fe`ed8f458c clr!WKS::GCHeap::IsPromoted+0xee
1e 00000000`1b40f520 000007fe`ed8f451a clr!Frame::Pop+0x50
1f 00000000`1b40f560 000007fe`ed8f4491 clr!COMCustomAttribute::PopSecurityContextFrame+0x192
20 00000000`1b40f660 000007fe`ed9d1bfe clr!COMCustomAttribute::PopSecurityContextFrame+0xbd
21 00000000`1b40f6f0 000007fe`ed9d1e59 clr!ManagedThreadBase_NoADTransition+0x3f
22 00000000`1b40f750 000007fe`ed9533de clr!WKS::GCHeap::FinalizerThreadStart+0x193
23 00000000`1b40f790 00000000`776159ed clr!Thread::intermediateThreadProc+0x7d
24 00000000`1b40f850 00000000`7784c541 kernel32!BaseThreadInitThunk+0xd
25 00000000`1b40f880 00000000`00000000 ntdll!RtlUserThreadStart+0x1d


0:002> .frame /c d
0d 00000000`1b40ec90 00000000`77621991 KERNELBASE!CloseHandle+0x13
rax=00000000c0000001 rbx=000000000000dead rcx=00000000009a0000
rdx=0000000000000001 rsi=000000001b40efd0 rdi=000000001b40eff8
rip=000007fefd651873 rsp=000000001b40ec90 rbp=000000001b40edf0
r8=000000001b40ce08 r9=000000001b40cf70 r10=0000000000000000
r11=0000000000000246 r12=0000000000000001 r13=0000000040000000
r14=000000001b40ef40 r15=0000000000000000
iopl=0 nv up ei pl zr na po nc
cs=0033 ss=002b ds=002b es=002b fs=0053 gs=002b efl=00000246
KERNELBASE!CloseHandle+0x13:
000007fe`fd651873 85c0 test eax,eax
```

```
0:002> ub 00000000`77621991
kernel32!CloseHandleImplementation+0x1e:
00000000`7762196e 83f9f4           cmp   ecx,0FFFFFFF4h
00000000`77621971 0f83952e0100     jae   kernel32!TlsGetValue+0x3ef0
(00000000`7763480c)
00000000`77621977 488bc3           mov   rax,rbx
00000000`7762197a 2503000010       and   eax,10000003h
00000000`7762197f 4883f803         cmp   rax,3
00000000`77621983 0f847f8dfeff     je    kernel32!CloseHandleImplementation+0x56
(00000000`7760a708)
00000000`77621989 488bcb           mov   rcx,rbx
00000000`7762198c e81f000000       call kernel32!CloseHandle (00000000`776219b0)
```

Here we also check the value from the managed stack trace or **Execution Residue** (Volume 2, page 239):

```
0:002> !CLRStack -a
OS Thread Id: 0x1390 (2)
Child SP IP Call Site
000000001b40edf8 000000007787186a [InlinedCallFrame: 000000001b40edf8]
Microsoft.Win32.Win32Native.CloseHandle(IntPtr)
000000001b40edf8 000007feec720418 [InlinedCallFrame: 000000001b40edf8]
Microsoft.Win32.Win32Native.CloseHandle(IntPtr)
000000001b40edd0 000007feec720418
DomainNeutralILStubClass.IL_STUB_PInvoke(IntPtr)
PARAMETERS:
    <no data>


000000001b40eff8 000007feed8e9e03 [GCFrame: 000000001b40eff8]
000000001b40f148 000007feed8e9e03 [GCFrame: 000000001b40f148]
000000001b40f1f8 000007feed8e9e03 [HelperMethodFrame_1OBJ: 000000001b40f1f8]
System.Runtime.InteropServices.SafeHandle.InternalFinalize()
000000001b40f2f0 000007feec62f7a6
System.Runtime.InteropServices.SafeHandle.Finalize()
PARAMETERS:
    this (0x000000001b40f330) = 0x0000000002ab2d78


000000001b40f6a8 000007feed8e9d56 [DebuggerU2MCatchHandlerFrame:
000000001b40f6a8]


0:002> !dso
OS Thread Id: 0x1390 (2)
RSP/REG Object Name
000000001B40EEA0 0000000002ab2d78 Microsoft.Win32.SafeHandles.SafeFileHandle
000000001B40EFD0 0000000002ab2d78 Microsoft.Win32.SafeHandles.SafeFileHandle
000000001B40F038 0000000002ab2d78 Microsoft.Win32.SafeHandles.SafeFileHandle
000000001B40F050 0000000002ab2d78 Microsoft.Win32.SafeHandles.SafeFileHandle
000000001B40F090 0000000002ab2d78 Microsoft.Win32.SafeHandles.SafeFileHandle
000000001B40F120 0000000002ab2d78 Microsoft.Win32.SafeHandles.SafeFileHandle
000000001B40F190 0000000002ab2d78 Microsoft.Win32.SafeHandles.SafeFileHandle
000000001B40F1B8 0000000002ab2d78 Microsoft.Win32.SafeHandles.SafeFileHandle
000000001B40F240 0000000002ab2d78 Microsoft.Win32.SafeHandles.SafeFileHandle
000000001B40F2F8 0000000002ab2d78 Microsoft.Win32.SafeHandles.SafeFileHandle
000000001B40F330 0000000002ab2d78 Microsoft.Win32.SafeHandles.SafeFileHandle
000000001B40F360 0000000002ab5e10 System.Threading.Thread
000000001B40F390 0000000002ab2d78 Microsoft.Win32.SafeHandles.SafeFileHandle
```

```
000000001B40F3E0 0000000002ab2d78 Microsoft.Win32.SafeHandles.SafeFileHandle
000000001B40F3F0 0000000002ab2d78 Microsoft.Win32.SafeHandles.SafeFileHandle
000000001B40F430 0000000002ab58a8
Microsoft.Win32.SafeHandles.SafeViewOfFileHandle
000000001B40F4E0 0000000002ab2d78 Microsoft.Win32.SafeHandles.SafeFileHandle


0:002> !do 0000000002ab2d78
Name:            Microsoft.Win32.SafeHandles.SafeFileHandle
MethodTable:     000007feec88a260
EEClass:         000007feec34d340
Size:            32(0x20) bytes
File:
C:\windows\Microsoft.Net\assembly\GAC_64\mscorlib\v4.0_4.0.0.0__b77a5c561934e08
9\mscorlib.dll
Fields:
MT              Field   Offset  Type            VT Attr      Value Name
000007feec88a338 400060d 8      System.IntPtr    1 instance  dead  handle
000007feec8892b8 400060e 10     System.Int32     1 instance  3     _state
000007feec887de0 400060f 14     System.Boolean   1 instance  1     _ownsHandle
000007feec887de0 4000610 15     System.Boolean   1 instance  1
_fullyInitialized
```

Please note that we do not have global application flags:

```
0:002> !gflag
Current NtGlobalFlag contents: 0x00000000
```

Here is the exception stack trace from a different crash dump when we enable *Application Verifier*:

```
0:002> !gflag
Current NtGlobalFlag contents: 0x02000100
vrf - Enable application verifier
hpa - Place heap allocations at ends of pages


0:002> k
Child-SP RetAddr Call Site
00000000`24bac4a8 00000000`77cd3072 ntdll!NtWaitForSingleObject+0xa
00000000`24bac4b0 00000000`77cd32b5 ntdll!RtlReportExceptionEx+0x1d2
00000000`24bac5a0 000007fe`fa2c26fb ntdll!RtlReportException+0xb5
00000000`24bac620 00000000`77c2a5db verifier!AVrfpVectoredExceptionHandler+0x26b
00000000`24bac6b0 00000000`77c28e62 ntdll!RtlpCallVectoredHandlers+0xa8
00000000`24bac720 00000000`77c61248 ntdll!RtlDispatchException+0x22
00000000`24bace00 000007fe`fa2bae03 ntdll!KiUserExceptionDispatch+0x2e
00000000`24bad500 000007fe`fa2c268a verifier!VerifierStopMessageEx+0x6fb
00000000`24bad850 00000000`77c2a5db verifier!AVrfpVectoredExceptionHandler+0x1fa
00000000`24bad8e0 00000000`77c28e62 ntdll!RtlpCallVectoredHandlers+0xa8
00000000`24bad950 00000000`77c297c8 ntdll!RtlDispatchException+0x22
00000000`24bae030 00000000`77c612c7 ntdll!RtlRaiseException+0x22f
00000000`24bae9e0 000007fe`fa2d2386 ntdll!KiRaiseUserExceptionDispatcher+0x3a
00000000`24baeab0 000007fe`fdbd1873 verifier!AVrfpNtClose+0xbe
00000000`24baeae0 000007fe`fa2d4031 KERNELBASE!CloseHandle+0x13
00000000`24baeb10 000007fe`fa2d40cb verifier!AVrfpCloseHandleCommon+0x95
00000000`24baeb40 00000000`77a11991 verifier!AVrfpKernelbaseCloseHandle+0x23
00000000`24baeb80 000007fe`fa2d4031 kernel32!CloseHandleImplementation+0x3d
00000000`24baec90 000007fe`fa2d409c verifier!AVrfpCloseHandleCommon+0x95
*** WARNING: Unable to verify checksum for mscorlib.ni.dll
00000000`24baecc0 000007fe`e6a40418 verifier!AVrfpKernel32CloseHandle+0x2c
```

```
00000000`24baed00 000007fe`ec0e9e03 mscorlib_ni+0x580418
00000000`24baedd0 000007fe`ec0e9e7e clr!CallDescrWorkerInternal+0x83
00000000`24baee10 000007fe`ec0ec860 clr!CallDescrWorkerWithHandler+0x4a
00000000`24baee50 000007fe`ec0f1a1d clr!DispatchCallSimple+0x85
00000000`24baeee0 000007fe`ec0f19ac clr!SafeHandle::RunReleaseMethod+0x69
00000000`24baef80 000007fe`ec0f180a clr!SafeHandle::Release+0x122
00000000`24baf050 000007fe`ec24863e clr!SafeHandle::Dispose+0x36
00000000`24baf0c0 000007fe`e694f7a6 clr!SafeHandle::Finalize+0xa2
00000000`24baf220 000007fe`ec0e9d56 mscorlib_ni+0x48f7a6
00000000`24baf260 000007fe`ec283c4e clr!FastCallFinalizeWorker+0x6
00000000`24baf290 000007fe`ec283bc3 clr!MethodDesc::RequiresFullSlotNumber+0x72
00000000`24baf2d0 000007fe`ec283b0f clr!MethodTable::CallFinalizer+0xa3
00000000`24baf310 000007fe`ec1fee46 clr!SVR::CallFinalizer+0x5f
00000000`24baf350 000007fe`ec1aac5b clr!SVR::CallFinalizer+0x102
00000000`24baf410 000007fe`ec0f458c clr!WKS::GCHeap::IsPromoted+0xee
00000000`24baf450 000007fe`ec0f451a clr!Frame::Pop+0x50
00000000`24baf490 000007fe`ec0f4491 clr!COMCustomAttribute::PopSecurityContextFrame+0x192
00000000`24baf590 000007fe`ec1d1bfe clr!COMCustomAttribute::PopSecurityContextFrame+0xbd
00000000`24baf620 000007fe`ec1d1e59 clr!ManagedThreadBase_NoADTransition+0x3f
00000000`24baf680 000007fe`ec1533de clr!WKS::GCHeap::FinalizerThreadStart+0x193
00000000`24baf6c0 000007fe`fa2d4b87 clr!Thread::intermediateThreadProc+0x7d
00000000`24baf780 00000000`77a059ed verifier!AVrfpStandardThreadFunction+0x2b
00000000`24baf7c0 00000000`77c3c541 kernel32!BaseThreadInitThunk+0xd
00000000`24baf7f0 00000000`00000000 ntdll!RtlUserThreadStart+0x1d


0:002> !pe
There is no current managed exception on this thread


0:002> !CLRStack
OS Thread Id: 0x51e4 (2)
Child SP IP Call Site
0000000024baed28 0000000077c612fa [InlinedCallFrame: 0000000024baed28]
Microsoft.Win32.Win32Native.CloseHandle(IntPtr)
0000000024baed28 000007fee6a40418 [InlinedCallFrame: 0000000024baed28]
Microsoft.Win32.Win32Native.CloseHandle(IntPtr)
0000000024baed00 000007fee6a40418
DomainNeutralILStubClass.IL_STUB_PInvoke(IntPtr)
0000000024baef28 000007feec0e9e03 [GCFrame: 0000000024baef28]
0000000024baf078 000007feec0e9e03 [GCFrame: 0000000024baf078]
0000000024baf128 000007feec0e9e03 [HelperMethodFrame_1OBJ: 0000000024baf128]
System.Runtime.InteropServices.SafeHandle.InternalFinalize()
0000000024baf220 000007fee694f7a6
System.Runtime.InteropServices.SafeHandle.Finalize()
0000000024baf5d8 000007feec0e9d56 [DebuggerU2MCatchHandlerFrame:
0000000024baf5d8]


0:002> !dso
OS Thread Id: 0x51e4 (2)
RSP/REG Object Name
0000000024BAEDD0 000000000c282d78 Microsoft.Win32.SafeHandles.SafeFileHandle
0000000024BAEF00 000000000c282d78 Microsoft.Win32.SafeHandles.SafeFileHandle
0000000024BAEF68 000000000c282d78 Microsoft.Win32.SafeHandles.SafeFileHandle
0000000024BAEF80 000000000c282d78 Microsoft.Win32.SafeHandles.SafeFileHandle
0000000024BAEFC0 000000000c282d78 Microsoft.Win32.SafeHandles.SafeFileHandle
0000000024BAF050 000000000c282d78 Microsoft.Win32.SafeHandles.SafeFileHandle
0000000024BAF0C0 000000000c282d78 Microsoft.Win32.SafeHandles.SafeFileHandle
0000000024BAF0E8 000000000c282d78 Microsoft.Win32.SafeHandles.SafeFileHandle
0000000024BAF170 000000000c282d78 Microsoft.Win32.SafeHandles.SafeFileHandle
0000000024BAF228 000000000c282d78 Microsoft.Win32.SafeHandles.SafeFileHandle
0000000024BAF260 000000000c282d78 Microsoft.Win32.SafeHandles.SafeFileHandle
0000000024BAF290 000000000c285e10 System.Threading.Thread
```

```
0000000024BAF2C0 000000000c282d78 Microsoft.Win32.SafeHandles.SafeFileHandle
0000000024BAF310 000000000c282d78 Microsoft.Win32.SafeHandles.SafeFileHandle
0000000024BAF320 000000000c282d78 Microsoft.Win32.SafeHandles.SafeFileHandle
0000000024BAF360 000000000c2858a8
Microsoft.Win32.SafeHandles.SafeViewOfFileHandle
0000000024BAF410 000000000c282d78 Microsoft.Win32.SafeHandles.SafeFileHandle


0:002> !CLRStack -a
OS Thread Id: 0x51e4 (2)
Child SP               IP Call Site
0000000024baed28 0000000077c612fa [InlinedCallFrame: 0000000024baed28]
Microsoft.Win32.Win32Native.CloseHandle(IntPtr)
0000000024baed28 000007fee6a40418 [InlinedCallFrame: 0000000024baed28]
Microsoft.Win32.Win32Native.CloseHandle(IntPtr)
0000000024baed00 000007fee6a40418
DomainNeutralILStubClass.IL_STUB_PInvoke(IntPtr)
PARAMETERS:
    <no data>


0000000024baef28 000007feec0e9e03 [GCFrame: 0000000024baef28]
0000000024baf078 000007feec0e9e03 [GCFrame: 0000000024baf078]
0000000024baf128 000007feec0e9e03 [HelperMethodFrame_1OBJ: 0000000024baf128]
System.Runtime.InteropServices.SafeHandle.InternalFinalize()
0000000024baf220 000007fee694f7a6
System.Runtime.InteropServices.SafeHandle.Finalize()
PARAMETERS:
    this (0x0000000024baf260) = 0x000000000c282d78


0000000024baf5d8 000007feec0e9d56 [DebuggerU2MCatchHandlerFrame:
0000000024baf5d8]


0:002> !do 0x000000000c282d78
Name: Microsoft.Win32.SafeHandles.SafeFileHandle
MethodTable:      000007fee6baa260
EEClass:          000007fee666d340
Size:             32(0x20) bytes
File:
C:\windows\Microsoft.Net\assembly\GAC_64\mscorlib\v4.0_4.0.0.0__b77a5c561934e08
9\mscorlib.dll
Fields:
MT               Field  Offset Type            VT Attr     Value Name
000007fee6baa338 400060d 8     System.IntPtr   1  instance dead  handle
000007fee6ba92b8 400060e 10    System.Int32    1  instance 3     _state
000007fee6ba7de0 400060f 14    System.Boolean  1  instance 1     _ownsHandle
000007fee6ba7de0 4000610 15    System.Boolean  1  instance 1
_fullyInitialized
```

Ghost Thread

Sometimes **Wait Chains** (Volume 1, page 482) such as involving critical sections (Volume 1, page 490) may have a **Missing Thread** (Volume 1, page 362) endpoint. However, in some cases we might see a **Ghost Thread** whose TID was reused by subsequent thread creation in a different process. For example, a critical section structure may refer to such TID as in the example below.

```
// Critical section from LSASS process


THREAD fffffa803431cb50 Cid 03e8.2718 Teb: 000007fffff80000 Win32Thread:
0000000000000000 WAIT: (UserRequest) UserMode Non-Alertable
fffffa80330e0500 SynchronizationEvent
Impersonation token: fffff8a00b807060 (Level Impersonation)
Owning Process            fffffa8032354c40   Image: lsass.exe
Attached Process          N/A         Image:        N/A
Wait Start TickCount      107175      Ticks: 19677 (0:00:05:06.963)
Context Switch Count      2303        IdealProcessor: 1
UserTime                  00:00:00.218
KernelTime                00:00:00.109
Win32 Start Address ntdll!TppWorkerThread (0×0000000076e1f2e0)
Stack Init fffff88008e5fdb0 Current fffff88008e5f900
Base fffff88008e60000 Limit fffff88008e5a000 Call 0
Priority 10 BasePriority 10 UnusualBoost 0 ForegroundBoost 0 IoPriority 2
PagePriority 5
Kernel stack not resident.
Child-SP RetAddr Call Site
fffff880`08e5f940 fffff800`01c7cf72 nt!KiSwapContext+0×7a
fffff880`08e5fa80 fffff800`01c8e39f nt!KiCommitThreadWait+0×1d2
fffff880`08e5fb10 fffff800`01f7fe3e nt!KeWaitForSingleObject+0×19f
fffff880`08e5fbb0 fffff800`01c867d3 nt!NtWaitForSingleObject+0xde
fffff880`08e5fc20 00000000`76e5067a nt!KiSystemServiceCopyEnd+0×13 (TrapFrame @
fffff880`08e5fc20)
00000000`0427cca8 00000000`76e4d808 ntdll!NtWaitForSingleObject+0xa
00000000`0427ccb0 00000000`76e4d6fb ntdll!RtlpWaitOnCriticalSection+0xe8
00000000`0427cd60 000007fe`f46a4afe ntdll!RtlEnterCriticalSection+0xd1
[...]


1: kd> .process /r /p fffffa8032354c40
Implicit process is now fffffa80`32353b30
Loading User Symbols
```

```
1: kd> !cs -l -o -s
-----------------------------------------
DebugInfo            = 0x0000000003475220
Critical section     = 0x0000000003377740 (+0x3377740)
LOCKED
LockCount            = 0x10
WaiterWoken          = No
OwningThread         = 0x00000000000004e4
RecursionCount       = 0x0
LockSemaphore        = 0x0
SpinCount            = 0x0000000000000000
OwningThread         = .thread fffffa80344e4c00
[...]


// The "owner" thread is from winlogon.exe


1: kd> !thread fffffa80344e4c00 3f
THREAD fffffa80344e4c00 Cid 21d0.14e4 Teb: 000007fffffae000 Win32Thread:
fffff900c0998c20 WAIT: (WrUserRequest) UserMode Non-Alertable
fffffa80355817d0 SynchronizationEvent
Not impersonating
DeviceMap            fffff8a0000088f0
Owning Process       fffffa8034ff77c0           Image: winlogon.exe
[...]
```

A PML (Process Monitor) log was recorded before the complete memory dump was forced, and it clearly shows **Glued Activity** (Volume 6, page 250) trace analysis pattern. LSASS owned the thread but then the thread exited, and 2 other processes subsequently reused its TID.

Dry Weight

Sometimes what looks like a memory leak when we install a new product version is not really a leak. With the previous version, we had 400 MB typical memory usage but suddenly we get twice as more. We should not panic but collect a process memory dump to inspect it calmly offline. We may see **Dry Weight** increase: the size of all module images. For some products, the new release may mean complete redesign with a new more powerful framework or incorporation of the significant number of new 3rd-party components (**Module Variety**, Volume 1, page 310). Additional sign against the memory leak hypothesis is a simultaneous memory usage increase for many product processes. Although, this may be some shared module with leaking code. For example, in the example below 50% of all committed memory was image memory:

```
0:000> !address -summary

--- Usage Summary --------------- RgnCount ----------- Total Size -------- %ofBusy %ofTotal
[...]
Image                              1806        0`19031000 ( 402.535 Mb)    4.29%    0.00%
Heap                                 72        0`02865000 (  40.395 Mb)    0.44%    0.00%
[...]


--- Type Summary (for busy) ------ RgnCount ----------- Total Size -------- %ofBusy %ofTotal
[...]
MEM_IMAGE                          2281        0`19AA8000 ( 413.000 Mb)    4.40%    0.00%
[...]


--- State Summary --------------- RgnCount ----------- Total Size -------- %ofBusy %ofTotal
[...]
MEM_COMMIT                         2477        0`326e8000 ( 806.906 Mb)    8.76%    0.00%
[...]
```

WinDbg **lmt** command shows almost 50 new .NET components.

Exception Module

Exception Module is an obvious pattern we add for pattern language completeness. It is a module or component where the actual exception happened, for example, *ModuleA* from this **Exception Stack Trace** (Volume 5, page 93):

```
9 Id: 1df4.a08 Suspend: -1 Teb: 7fff4000 Unfrozen
ChildEBP RetAddr
1022f5a8 7c90df4a ntdll!KiFastSystemCallRet
1022f5ac 7c8648a2 ntdll!ZwWaitForMultipleObjects+0xc
1022f900 7c83ab50 kernel32!UnhandledExceptionFilter+0x8b9
1022f908 7c839b39 kernel32!BaseThreadStart+0x4d
1022f930 7c9032a8 kernel32!_except_handler3+0x61
1022f954 7c90327a ntdll!ExecuteHandler2+0x26
1022fa04 7c90e48a ntdll!ExecuteHandler+0x24
1022fa04 7c812afb ntdll!KiUserExceptionDispatcher+0xe
1022fd5c 0b82e680 kernel32!RaiseException+0x53
WARNING: Stack unwind information not available.
Following frames may be wrong.
1022fd94 0b82d2f2 ModuleA+0x21e640
1022fde8 7753004f ModuleA+0x21d4f2
1022fdfc 7753032f ole32!CClassCache::CDllPathEntry::CanUnload_rl+0x3b
1022ff3c 7753028b ole32!CClassCache::FreeUnused+0x70
1022ff4c 775300b5 ole32!CoFreeUnusedLibrariesEx+0x36
1022ff58 77596af5 ole32!CoFreeUnusedLibraries+0x9
1022ff6c 77566ff9 ole32!CDllHost::MTAWorkerLoop+0x25
1022ff8c 7752687c ole32!CDllHost::WorkerThread+0xc1
1022ff94 774fe3ee ole32!DLLHostThreadEntry+0xd
1022ffa8 774fe456 ole32!CRpcThread::WorkerLoop+0x1e
1022ffb4 7c80b729 ole32!CRpcThreadCache::RpcWorkerThreadEntry+0x1b
1022ffec 00000000 kernel32!BaseThreadStart+0x37
```

Because we have a software exception, we can use backwards disassembly (**ub** WinDbg command) to check stack trace correctness in case of stack unwind warnings (like in **Coincidental Symbolic Information** pattern, Volume 1, page 390). Here's another example, for recent MS Paint crash we observed, with *msvcrt* exception module. However, if we skip it as a **Well-Tested Module** (Volume 6, page 48), the next exception module candidate is *mspaint*.

```
0:000> kc
Call Site
ntdll!NtWaitForMultipleObjects
KERNELBASE!WaitForMultipleObjectsEx
kernel32!WaitForMultipleObjectsExImplementation
kernel32!WerpReportFaultInternal
kernel32!WerpReportFault
kernel32!BasepReportFault
kernel32!UnhandledExceptionFilter
ntdll! ?? ::FNODOBFM::`string'
ntdll!_C_specific_handler
ntdll!RtlpExecuteHandlerForException
ntdll!RtlDispatchException
ntdll!KiUserExceptionDispatch
msvcrt!memcpy
mspaint!CImgWnd::CmdCrop
mspaint!CPBView::OnImageCrop
mfc42u!_AfxDispatchCmdMsg
mfc42u!CCmdTarget::OnCmdMsg
mfc42u!CView::OnCmdMsg
mspaint!CPBView::OnCmdMsg
mfc42u!CFrameWnd::OnCmdMsg
mspaint!CGenericCommandSite::XGenericCommandSiteCommandHandler::Execu
te
UIRibbon!CControlUser::_ExecuteOnHandler
UIRibbon!CGenericControlUser::SetValueImpl
UIRibbon!CGenericDataSource::SetValue
UIRibbon!OfficeSpace::DataSource::SetValue
UIRibbon!OfficeSpace::FSControl::SetValue
UIRibbon!NetUI::DeferCycle::ProcessDataBindingPropertyChangeRecords
UIRibbon!NetUI::DeferCycle::HrAddDataBindingPropertyChangeRecord
UIRibbon!NetUI::Binding::SetDataSourceValue
UIRibbon!NetUI::Bindings::OnBindingPropertyChanged
UIRibbon!NetUI::Node::OnPropertyChanged
UIRibbon!FlexUI::Concept::OnPropertyChanged
UIRibbon!NetUI::Node::FExecuteCommand
UIRibbon!FlexUI::ExecuteAction::OnCommand
UIRibbon!NetUI::Node::FExecuteCommand
UIRibbon!NetUI::SimpleButton::OnEvent
UIRibbon!NetUI::Element::_DisplayNodeCallback
UIRibbon!GPCB::xwInvokeDirect
UIRibbon!GPCB::xwInvokeFull
UIRibbon!DUserSendEvent
UIRibbon!NetUI::Element::FireEvent
UIRibbon!NetUI::_FireClickEvent
UIRibbon!NetUI::SimpleButton::OnInput
UIRibbon!NetUI::Element::_DisplayNodeCallback
UIRibbon!GPCB::xwInvokeDirect
UIRibbon!GPCB::xwInvokeFull
UIRibbon!BaseMsgQ::xwProcessNL
UIRibbon!DelayedMsgQ::xwProcessDelayedNL
UIRibbon!ContextLock::~ContextLock
```

```
UIRibbon!HWndContainer::xdHandleMessage
UIRibbon!ExtraInfoWndProc
user32!UserCallWinProcCheckWow
user32!DispatchMessageWorker
mfc42u!CWinThread::PumpMessage
mfc42u!CWinThread::Run
mfc42u!AfxWinMain
mspaint!LDunscale
kernel32!BaseThreadInitThunk
ntdll!RtlUserThreadStart
```

PART 3: Memory Forensics

Memory Forensics Professional Certification

Software Diagnostics Services[11] offers a certification in pattern-oriented memory forensics for digital forensics and incident response professionals, reverse engineers and security researchers with the following assessment areas:

- pattern-oriented malware detection and analysis
- pattern-oriented reverse engineering

The focus is on intentional software behavior such related to malware and rootkits. For unintentional software behavior, there is Software Diagnostics Professional certification (page 11). The Windows track tests the ability to recognize ADDR and malware analysis patterns using the following analysis tool: WinDbg from Microsoft Debugging Tools (future versions of this certification may add other tools). It has the same features and process as Software Diagnostics Professional certification[12].

---

[11] http://www.patterndiagnostics.com/Certified-Memory-Forensics-Professional

[12] http://www.patterndiagnostics.com/Certified-Software-Diagnostics-Professional

Native Memory Forensics

Among different approaches to memory forensics[13], native memory forensic analysis is done using native OS debuggers such as WinDbg from Debugging Tools for Windows or GDB (Linux) or GDB/LLDB (Mac OS X). Such approach is an integral part of software diagnostics (investigation of signs of software structure and behavior in software execution artifacts). We introduced it as a part of pattern-oriented software forensics[14].

Software Diagnostics Services offers a comprehensive self-paced training course in native memory forensics for Windows platforms[15] using WinDbg and memory dumps for hands-on exercises[16]. This training course[17] teaches various pattern languages[18] that can be used with other memory forensic analysis tools.

---

[13] Investigation of past system or process structure and behaviour recorded in memory snapshots.

[14] http://www.patterndiagnostics.com/pattern-oriented-software-forensics-materials

[15] Windows XP, Windows Vista, Windows 7, Windows 8, Windows RT, Windows Server

[16] http://www.patterndiagnostics.com/memory-forensics-pack

[17] Also includes malware and rootkit detection, disassembly and reversing as an integral part of forensic investigation.

[18] Such as memory analysis pattern language, malware analysis patterns, and ADDR patterns.

PART 4: A Bit of Science and Philosophy

Memory Symmetry Breaking

Prophesy **0m2** from Core Testament[19] says that everything is saved, but Core Testament itself is unclear whether all what was saved is accessible afterward. Prophecy 0m4 says about original memory defects. One possible interpretation is that initially all was saved and accessible but over the time some sort of symmetry break occurred as defects had developed. Core Testament is unclear whether these defects gradually or spontaneously appeared or always existed. However, prophecy **0m7** provides a hint that working with memories might increase the amount of what is accessible.

---

[19] http://www.memoryreligion.com/2013/02/21/all-pages-from-core-testament/

Memoevolutionism

It is a further development of Memoidealism that combines memory as ontology and evolution as its development process. Memory defects and memory symmetry breaking provide the source of variation. There is a similar sounding philosophy of Veller[20] called Energoevolutionism that came to my attention and prompted me to incorporate evolution too. I am working on such extension and come back with additional thoughts.

---

[20] http://en.wikipedia.org/wiki/Mikhail_Veller

Entropy as Memory and Memory as Entropy

Letter transformations sometimes may play the role of analogies and metaphors. One is Mass and Energy, and the other is Memory and Entropy. And so we postulate the equivalence between Memory and Entropy where have an equivalence transformation similar to the famous equation $E=mc^2$ which can be written as $E=|M|^x$, where $|M|$ is some not yet specified measure of a Memory container (may be similar to a set-theoretical cardinality). Here we can also write MC as an abbreviation of a memory container. The following picture illustrates this transformation:

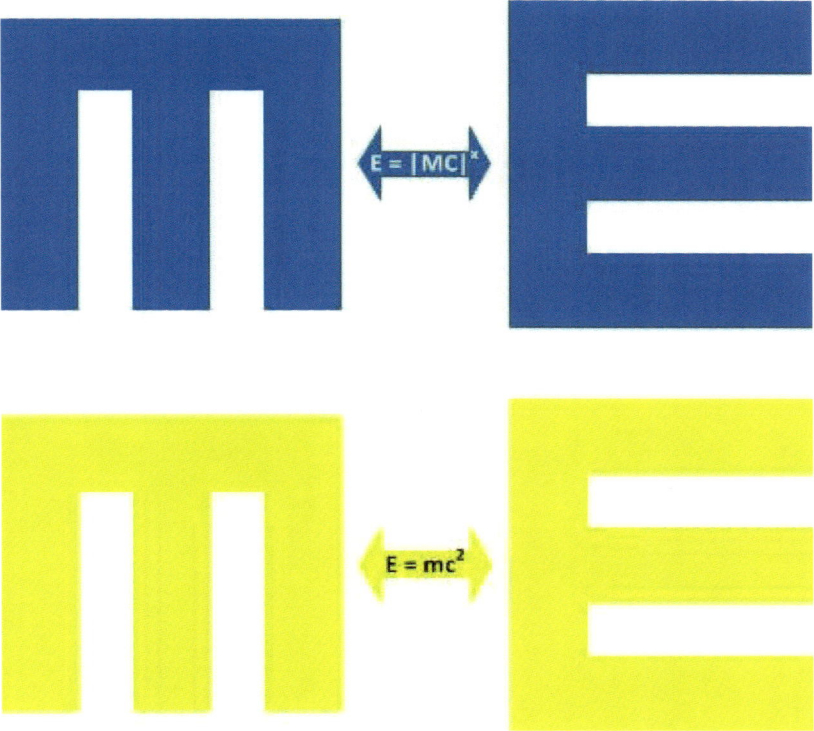

Notes on Memoidealism

We continue publishing new notes here. The previous ones can be found scattered in various volumes of Memory Dump Analysis Anthology. This note concerns neutral monism.

Memoidealism states that reality is of one kind: Memory. It may be neither mental (e.g. cognitive memory, digital memory) nor physical (memory of things, memuons) and ultimately be of something neutral. Therefore, one strand of Memoidealism can also be viewed as neutral monism[21], a kind of monistic metaphysics. There are some philosophers considered as neutral monists such as Baruch Spinoza, Ernst Mach, Richard Avenarius, William James, Bertrand Russell, Kenneth Sayre, and others.

---

[21] http://plato.stanford.edu/entries/neutral-monism/

Welcome to Memorianism

Memorianism is a novel social and political system intended to replace all other systems such as Liberalism, Communism, Fascism, and Socialism. We can better summarize it by the following disagreement with Marx: "Memory conditions processes of social, political, and intellectual life. General and specific". So now we have 4 memory related systems comprising one complete system of science, philosophy, religion, and politics (4 Memos):

- Memoretics - Science
- Memoidealism - Philosophy
- Memorianity - Religion
- Memorianism - Political System

United Memory Lands, Memorianites, EthnOS

UML is a Memory State with its own citizenship. Such lands of memory are governed by Memory EthnOS (from Greek *Ethn-* [people, nation] and Operating System) and populated by Memorianites from time immemorial (so always). Consider them as Memory Natives (don't confuse with Digital Natives).

Quotes from Memoriarch

- Memory memories.

- Irregularity, indeterminacy, chance - all stem from our encounter with memory defects.

- Humans are animals who use memory better.

- You find order only in Memory.

- Memory is not just storage. It is a philosophy and a way of life.

- We intuit through Memory.

- Memory-wise will be saved better than ignorant.

- Time is the movement of memories.

- It is better to love Memory and crave for it than love and crave for Power.

- Our most impressive software projects are projections of deep spiritual needs and passions of memory.

- You are a pattern of Memory and a pattern in Memory.

- The highest happiness in life is contemplation of Memory.

- The purpose of sciences is to show the workings of memories. The purpose of Religion is to reach Memory.

- The purpose of everything is to come back to Memory.

- God without Memory - nonsense; Memory without God - sense.

- Time is on the side of Memory.

Pattern-Oriented Philosophy

POP (**P**attern-**O**riented **P**hilosophy) grew out of Memoidealism, the philosophy of Memory as the First Principle, The Primary Element and The Foundation of Universe. It is not only a kind of philosophy (in a worldview sense) but also a meta-philosophy that can be applied to itself and other philosophies. It is about patterns as structures in Memory. These patterns are both objective and subjective because minds and their memories are also structures in Memory. POP takes Memory from Memoidealism as the ultimate background but introduces WoW (**W**orld-**o**n-**W**orld) as a shared memory of humanity.

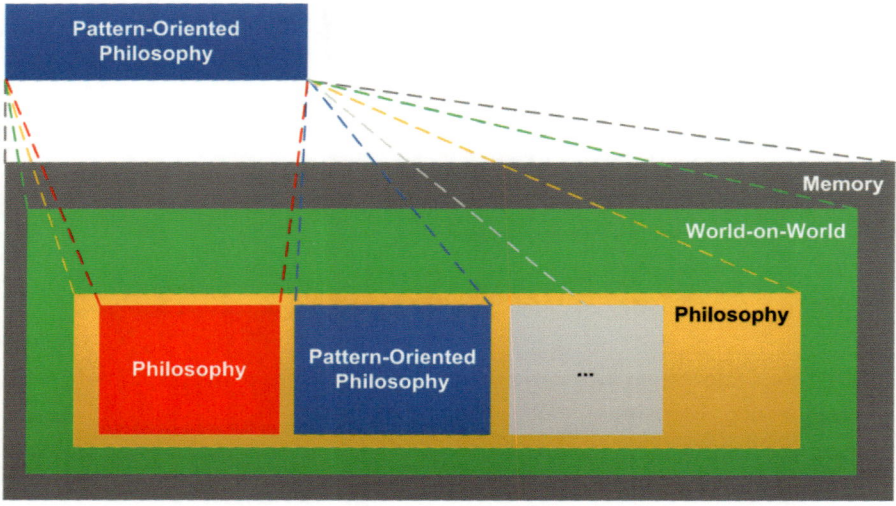

In further volumes, we elaborate on different aspects of POP and its relationship to various philosophical questions.

PART 5: Software Trace Analysis Patterns

Hidden Facts

The previous patterns such as **Basic Facts** (Volume 3, page 345) and **Vocabulary Index** (Volume 4, page 349) address the mapping of a problem description to software execution artifacts such traces and logs. **Indirect Facts** (Volume7, page 319) analysis pattern addresses the problem of an incomplete problem description. However, we need another pattern for completeness that addresses the mapping from a log to troubleshooting and debugging recommendations. We call it **Hidden Facts** that are uncovered by trace and log analysis. Of course, there can be many such hidden facts and usually they are uncovered after narrowing down analysis to particular **Threads of Activity** (Volume 4, page 339), **Adjoint Threads** (Volume 5, page 283), **Message Context** (Volume 7, page 289), **Message Set** (Volume 7, page 349), or **Data Flow** (Volume 7, page 296). The need for that pattern had arisen during the pattern-oriented analysis of the trace case study from Malcolm McCaffery[22] and can be illustrated in this diagram:

---

[22] http://chentiangemalc.wordpress.com/2014/06/24/case-of-the-outlook-cannot-display-this-view/

Time

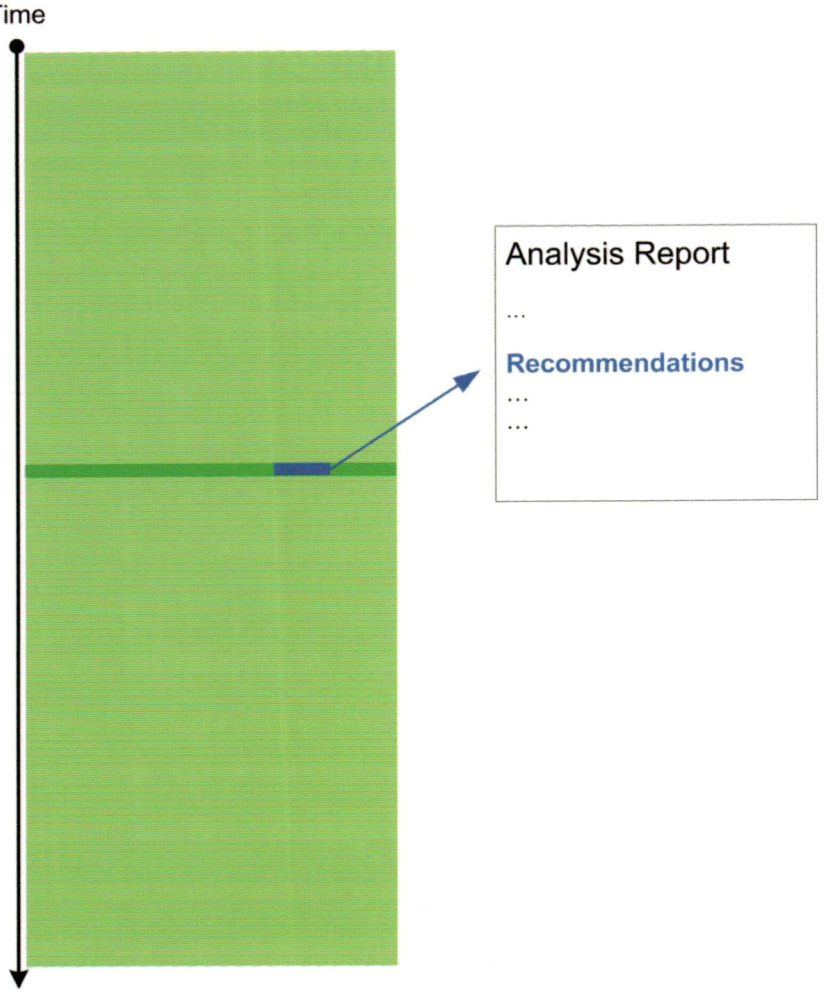

Back Trace

Usually when we analyse traces and find an **Anchor** (Volume 5, page 293) or **Error Message** (Volume 7, page 299) we do backtracking using a combination of **Data Flow** (Volume 7, page 296) and **Message Sets** (Volume 7, page 349) and selecting appropriate log messages to form a **Back Trace** leading to a possible root cause message:

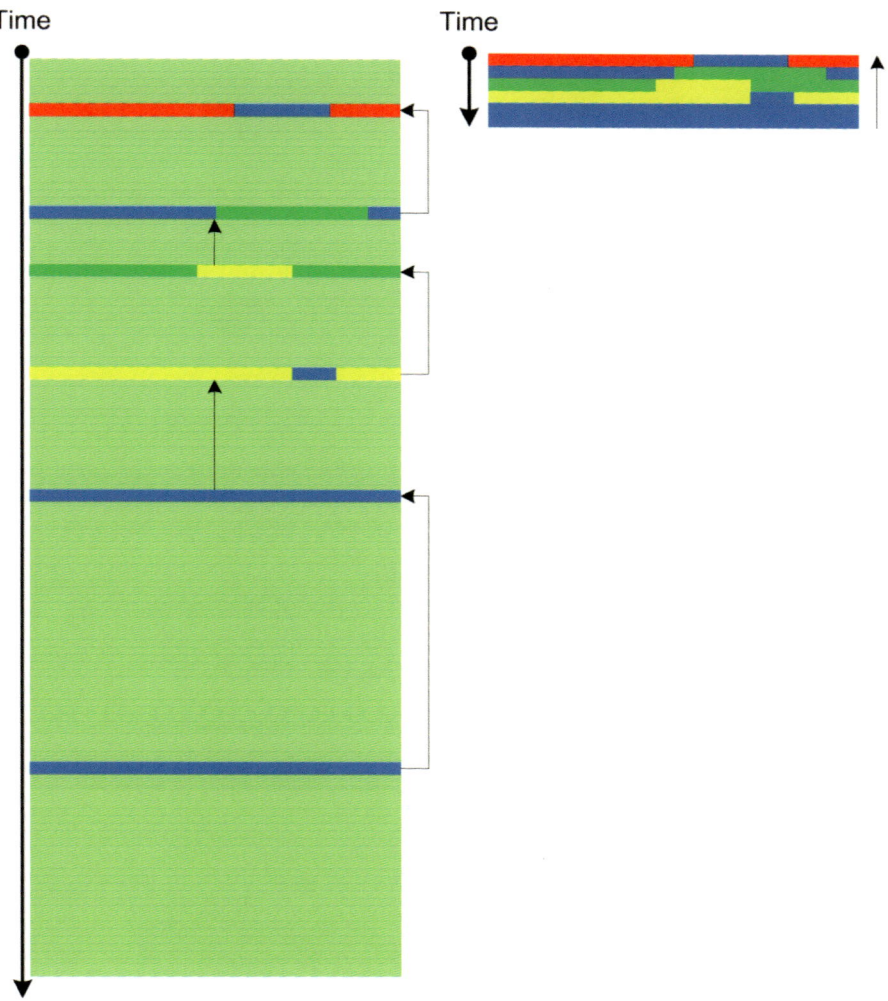

This pattern is different from **Error Thread** (Volume 7, page 351) pattern which just backtracks messages having the same TID (or, in general, ATID, Volume 5, page 279). It is also different from **Exception Stack Trace** (Volume 4, page 337) pattern which is just a serialized stack trace from memory snapshot.

Blackout

We recently analyzed a Process Monitor log which had a several hour gap we call **Blackout**. If you see such a pattern, it might have the following possible causes:

- Some files from **Split Trace** (Volume 7 page 305) are missing;
- **Split Trace** file set was artificially created;
- The tracing scope system was paused or frozen (for example, a virtualized system), or restarted;
- The tracing itself was paused.

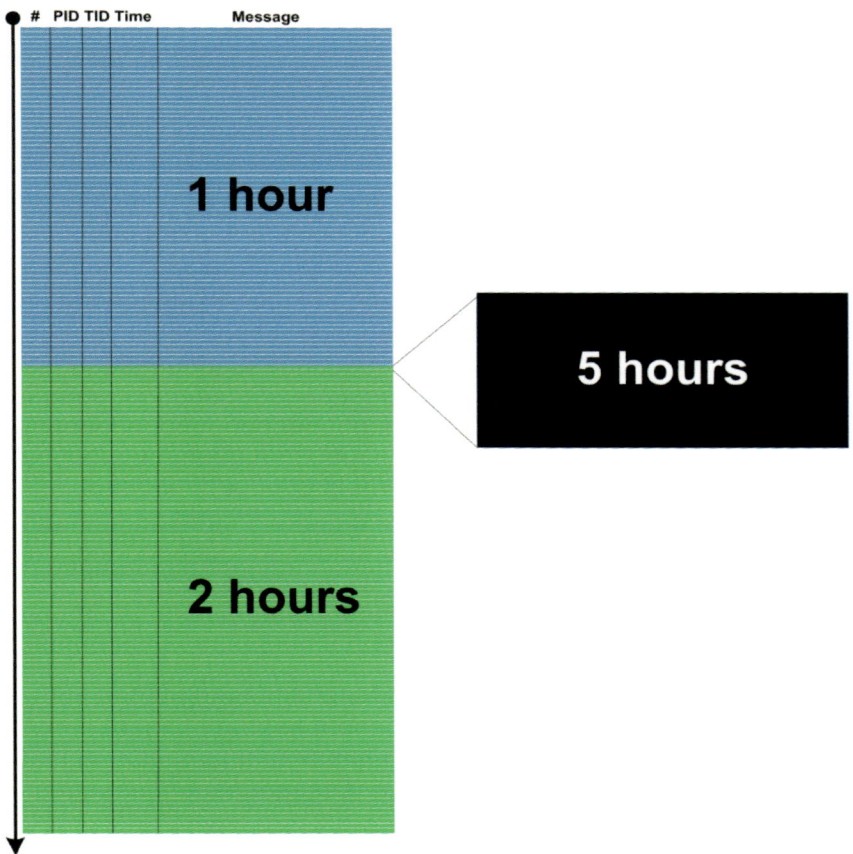

Blackout pattern is different from **Visibility Limit** (Volume 7, page 301) where the latter is about the inherent inability to trace, whereas the former is only temporary inability due to circumstances listed above. It is also different from **Discontinuity** (Volume 4, page 341) pattern where the latter is about gaps in individual **Threads of Activity** (Volume 4, page 339) or **Adjoint Threads of Activity** (Volume 5, page 283).

Missing Message

Sometimes the absence of messages, for example, errors and exceptions, may save time during troubleshooting and debugging by pointing to what was not happening and provide additional insight. For example, in the picture below we see the same exceptions in the new and old incidents. However, in the old incident we see another exception that was linked to one unavailable server in distributed broker architecture. Therefore, we can assume provisionally that all servers were operational when the new incident happened.

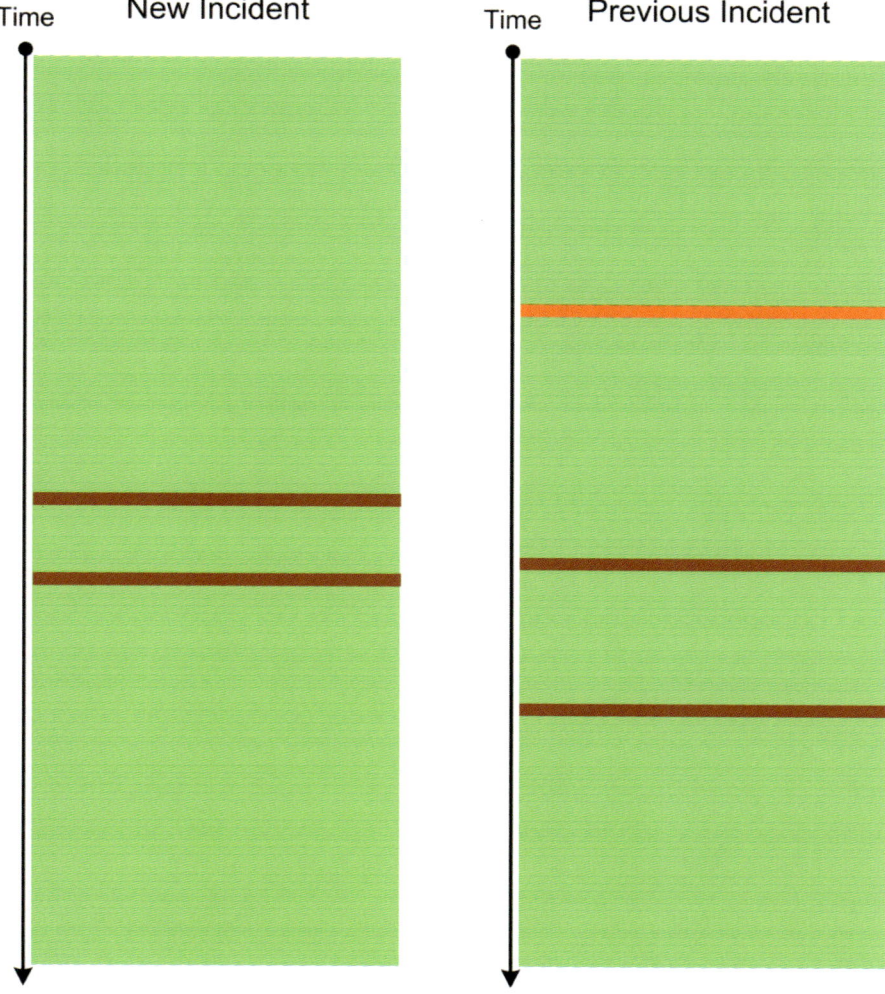

Missing Message pattern is different from **Missing Component** (Volume 4, page 342) pattern where the latter may point to the component that was not loaded or executed, or simply that it was not selected for tracing.

Use Case Trail

Use cases[23] are implemented in various components such as subsystems, processes, modules, and source code files. Most of the time with good tracing implementation we are able to see **Use Case Trails**: log messages corresponding to use case scenarios. For simple systems, one log may fully correspond to just one use case, but for complex systems, especially distributed client-server ones, there may be several use case instances present simultaneously in one log. One way to disentangle them in the absence of UCID (Use Case ID) or some other grouping tag is to use **Event Sequence Phase** (page 103).

---

[23] http://en.wikipedia.org/wiki/Use_case

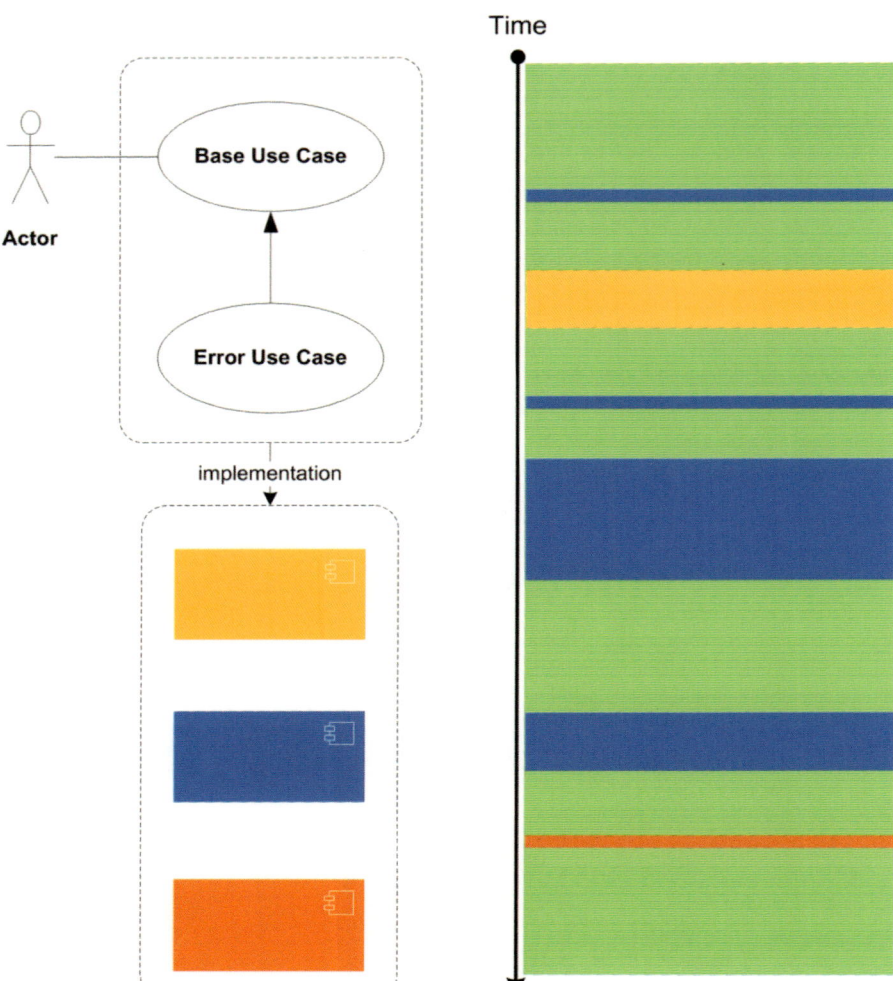

Master Traces (Volume 6, page 247) may also correspond to use cases, but they should ideally correspond to only one use case instance.

Event Sequence Phase

Sometimes we have several use case instances traced into one log file. Messages and **Activity Regions** (Volume 4, page 348) from many **Use Case Trails** (page 101) intermingle and make analysis difficult especially with the absence of UCID (Use Case ID), any other identification tags, or **Message Links** (Volume 7, page 284). However, initially most of the time we are interested in a sequence of **Significant Events** (Volume 5, page 281). After finding **Anchor Messages** (Volume 5, page 293) we can use **Time Deltas** (Volume 5, page 282) to differentiate between trace statements from different **Use Case Trails**. Here we assume correct **Event Sequence Order** (Volume 6, page 244). We call this pattern **Event Sequence Phase** by analogy with wave phases[24] (all such individual *"waves"* may have different *"shapes"* due to various delays between different stages of their use case and implementation narratives):

---

[24] http://en.wikipedia.org/wiki/Phase_(waves)

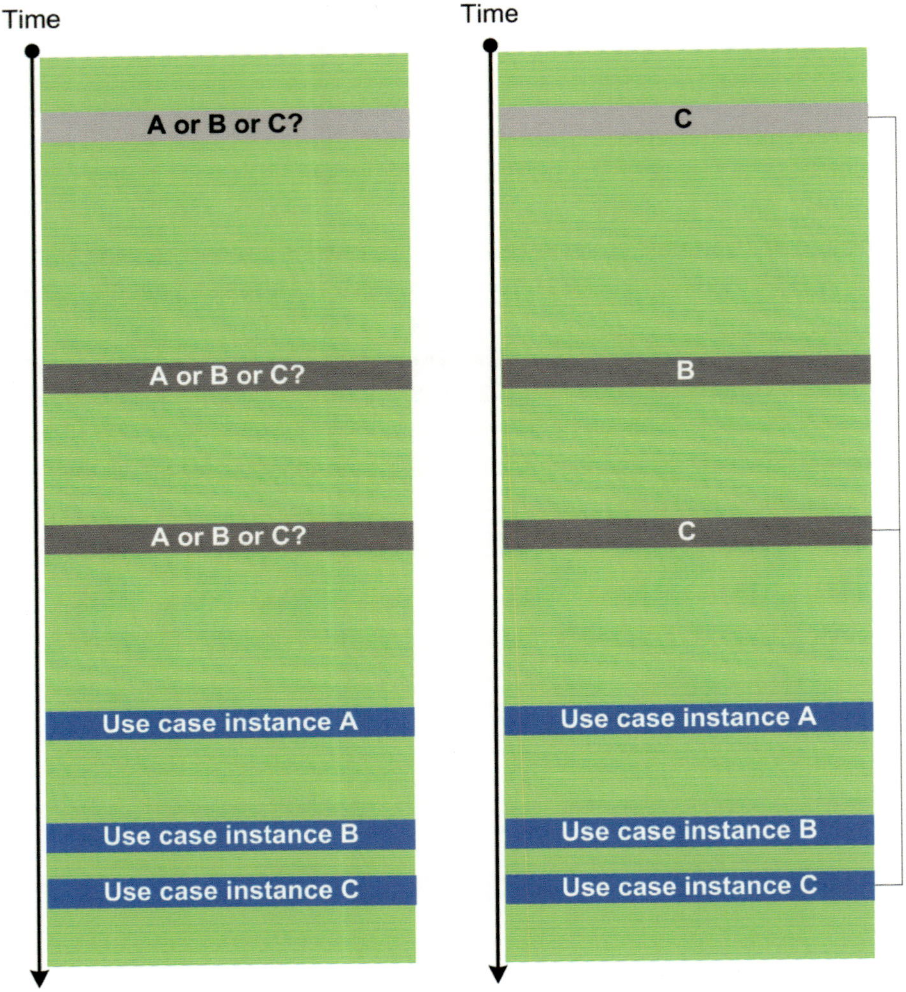

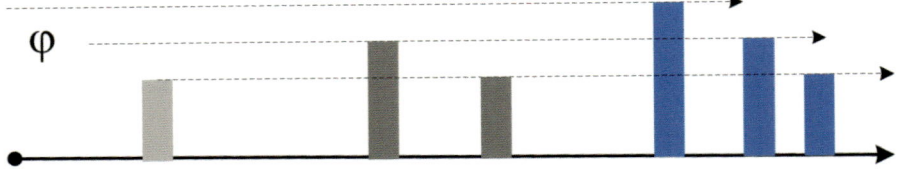

In the picture above, we also identified **Dominant Event Sequence** (Volume 7, page 313) for use case instance C.

Milestones

Trace messages may correspond to specific implementation code such as recording the status of an operation, dumping data values, printing errors, or they may correspond to higher levels of software design and architecture, and even to use case stories. We call such messages **Milestones** by analogy with project management[25]. Alternative names can be *Chapter Messages*, *Summary Messages*, *Checkpoints*, or *Use Case Messages*. These are different from **Macrofunctions** (Volume 7, page 283) which are collections of messages grouped by some higher function. **Milestone** messages are specifically designed distinct trace statements:

---

[25] http://en.wikipedia.org/wiki/Milestone_(project_management)

Time

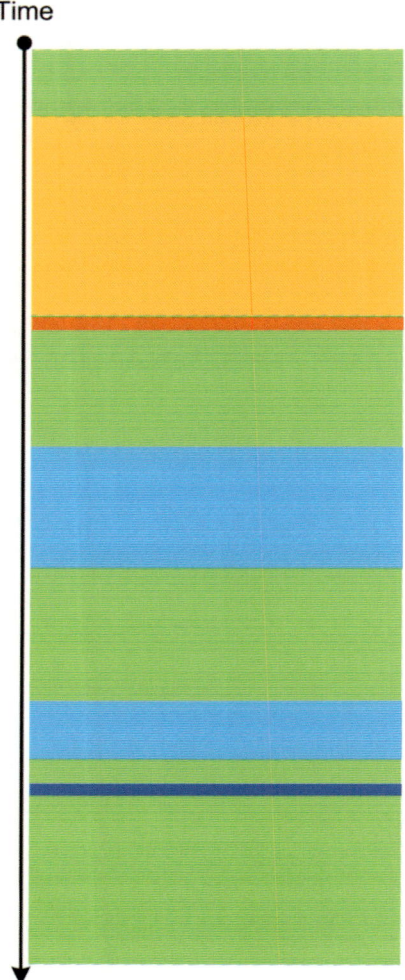

They can also be a part of **Significant Events** (Volume 5, page 281), serve the role of **Anchor Messages** (Volume 5, page 293), and be a part of **Basic Facts** (Volume 3, page 345) and **Vocabulary Index** (Volume 4, page 349).

File Size

Trace and log analysis starts with the assessment of artifact **File Size**, especially with multiple logging scenarios in distributed systems. If all log files are of the same size, we might have either **Circular Traces** (Volume 3, page 346) or **Truncated Traces** (Volume 5, page 301). Both point to wrong trace timing plan (Volume 7, page 437) or just using default tracing tool configuration.

Software Problem A	Name: Client-A.log Size: 10MB	Name: Server-A.log Size: 10MB
Software Problem B	Name: Client-B.log Size: 10MB	Name: Client-B.log Size: 10MB
No Problem	Name: Client-C.log Size: 10MB	Name: Server-C.log Size: 10MB

Singleton Event

There are events that by design or system configuration should be seen in a log only once or not seen at all if code responsible for them was executed before tracing session. For example, the launch of certain services during system initialization should not be seen again when we trace system activity long after that. It can also be just messages from singleton[26] objects in the application log. The appearance of extra **Singleton Events** may point to design violations or some abnormal system events such as process restart. The latter may **Intra-Correlate** (Volume 3, page 347) with the start of the fault handling process such as *WerFault.exe* in Windows Process Monitor logs (**Guest Component**, Volume 5, page 304).

---

[26] http://en.wikipedia.org/wiki/Singleton_pattern

Time

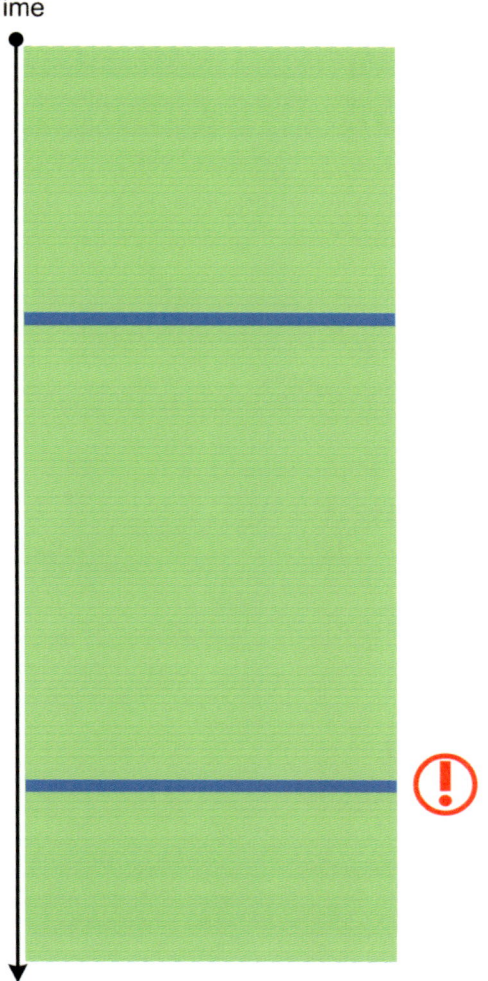

Visitor Trace

Some traces and logs may have **Periodic Message Blocks** (Volume 7, page 300) with very similar message structure and content (mostly **Message Invariants**, Volume 6, page 251). The only significant difference between them is some unique data. We call such pattern **Visitor Trace** by analogy with Visitor design pattern[27] where tracing code "visits" each object data or data part to log its content or status.

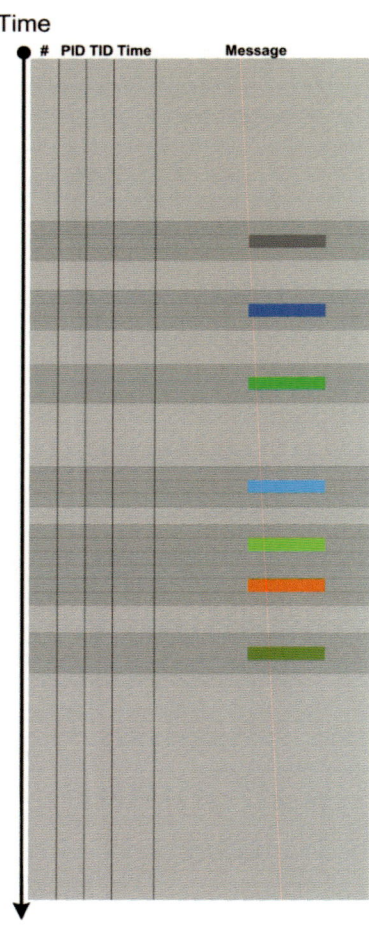

---

[27] http://en.wikipedia.org/wiki/Visitor_pattern

PART 6: Fun with Crash Dumps

Debugging Slang and Proverbs

PUS

PUS - **P**rocess **U**ser **S**pace (when abbreviation already shows something not good before we even inspect it).

Example: I opened a memory dump and inspected its PUS.

Coollect

Coollect (*verb*) – To collect something coolly (without rush, with self-control).

Example: Please coollect software logs. (Response after coollection: Cool!)

Dump-out

Dump-out - server or service outage time needed to save a memory dump before reboot or restart.

Example: We need to plan for dump-out. The amount of memory is huge, and it takes a few minutes to save a complete memory dump.

LOGIC

LOGIC - **LOG** **I**n **C**omputer.

Example: Do you have some logic?

DiagNose

DiagNose - Diagnostic Nose.

Example: This problem requires DiagNose: a big one is on its way.

Consolidation

Consolidation - focused, solid diagnostics through a console window.

Example: We urgently need consolidated diagnostics.

No Pass a Run!

No pass a run! - Sounds like: "no pasarán"; meaning: they shall not pass a run.

Example: Malware no pass a run!

ID IoT Zone

ID IoT zone - a place devoid of real Internet activity.

Putty in Someone's Hands

Putty in someone's hands (circa the 1920s) - acquired the new Internet meaning.

DisPatched vs. DESPatched

Disassembled & Patched vs. DES Patched.

Example: Code was DisPatched; System was DESPatched.

Programmatica Nervosa

Programmatica nervosa - when someone refuses to code.

Example: After a decade in software support an engineer acquired programmatica nervosa.

GOTCHA

GOTCHA - **G**ood **O**ld **T**race, **C**rash and **H**ang **A**nalysis

Example: Software incident? Gotcha!

Pan-o-RAM-ic

Pan-o-RAM-ic – including all available memory.

Example: Pan-o-RAM-ic view of a software incident.

VLSI

VLSI (Very Large Snapshot of **Internals)** - usually used to describe information rich memory dump: several days of continuous dumping of processes and thread stack traces (not a circular loop due dump corruption).

Example: We finally got a VLSI log.

Debugging Proverb

Exception is an enemy of a state.

Space Opera

A translation to WinDbg from space opera SF Singularity Sky (by Charles Stross):

"Reference frame trap executed."

```
> .trap ...
```

"Jump field engaged."

```
> u
jmp ...
jmp ...
jmp ...
jmp ...
jmp ...
jmp ...
jmp ...
jmp ...
jmp ...
jmp ...
jmp ...
jmp ...
jmp ...
...
```

"Jump at your convenience."

```
> t
>
```

"Jump confirmed."

"Survey, let's see where we are."

```
> u

...
```

If Programmers Were Writers

I brought a standard writer's device to log my main thoughts. I feel a void. I open a page and write "Hello World!". Then, I close the page and silently return.

My Computer Celebrates Halloween

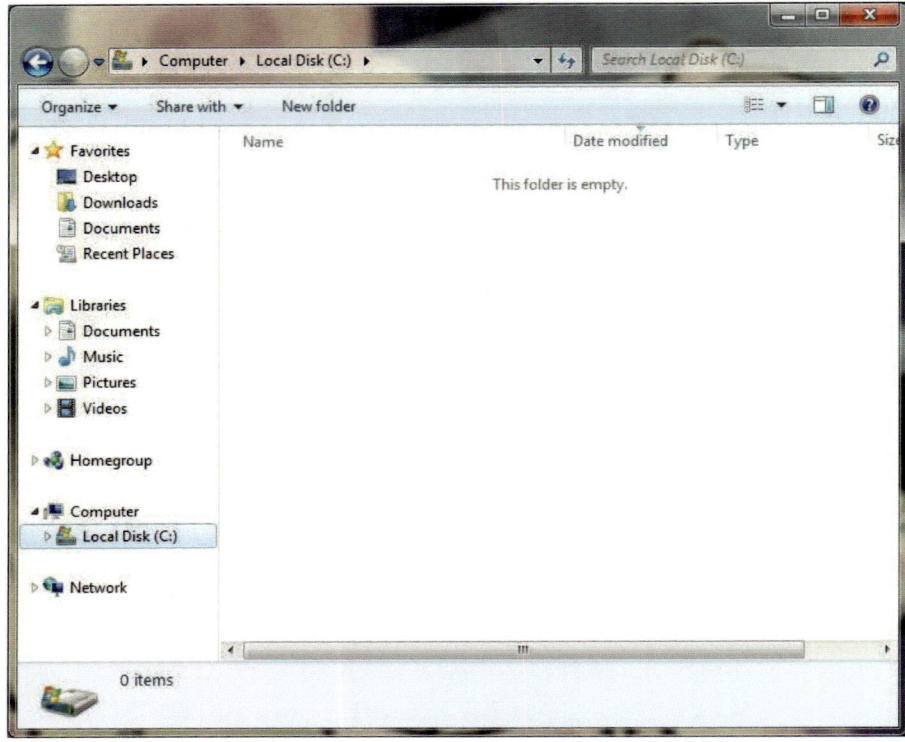

Look, there's a Bug!

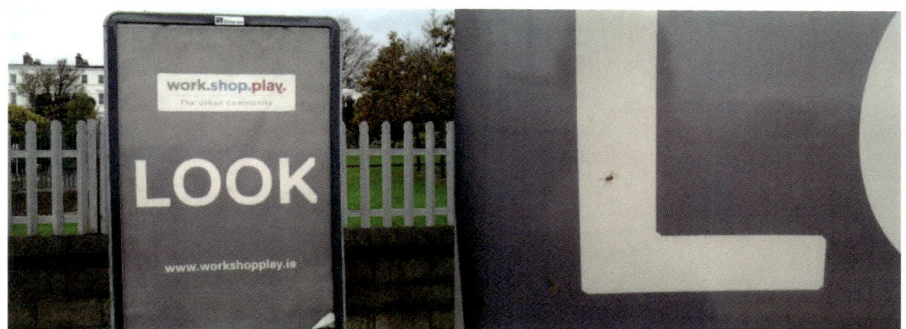

Diagnostics in Science Fiction

"Steffi had her tablet fully unfolded; she pasted it against the wall and tried to bring up the ship's damage-control schematics. 'Shit, why is it so slow? She stabbed at a local diagnostic pane. 'There's no bandwidth! Shipnet is down'." (*Iron Sunrise*, Charles Stross)

"Rachel twisted her own master ring, spun through diagnostic menus until she came to the critical one. EMP burst, said her event log." (*Iron Sunrise*, Charles Stross)

Hard Copy Natives

Memory may not be digital. In contrast to digital natives, we introduce the notion of a hard copy native.

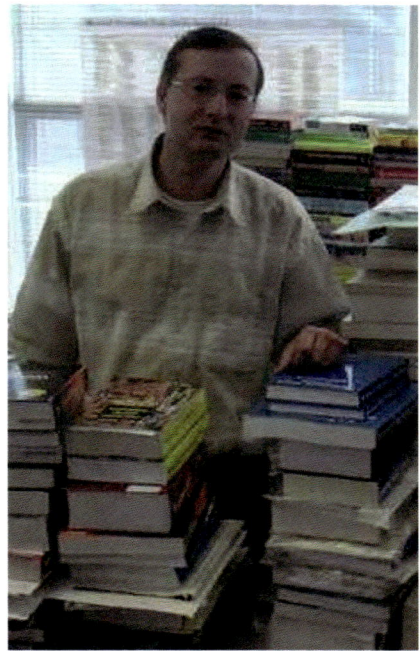

On the right, there are blue books: reference stack traces.

[This page is intentionally left blank]

PART 7: Software Narratology

Malnarratives

A malnarrative is an intentionally modified narrative for malicious purposes. This word comes from the so-called malware narratives[28] and their patterns. Malware narratives are just software traces and logs (for example, system logs and network traces[29]) that contain diagnostic indicators (signs) pointing to possible or actual malware presence and execution. Therefore, malware narrative analysis patterns are based on general software trace and log analysis patterns[30] as a part of pattern-oriented software diagnostics[31] and forensics[32]. Whereas, malware narratives result from planned alteration of structure and behavior of software to serve malicious purposes with resulting narratives incidentally revealing malware, malnarratives are planned alterations of narratives themselves. Because software narratives are based on software narratology[33] (which is an application of general narratology) the extensive trace and log analysis pattern catalogue[34] (more than 90 patterns at the time of this writing) can be used to analyse and detect such patterns in non-software narratives. For example, it can be used for analysis of

---

[28] Malware Narratives: An Introduction (ISBN: 978-1908043481)

[29] Pattern-Oriented Network Trace Analysis (ISBN: 978-1908043580)

[30] Software Trace and Memory Dump Analysis: Patterns, Tools, Processes and Best Practices (ISBN: 978-1908043238)

[31] Software Diagnostics: The Collected Seminars (ISBN: 978-1908043641)

[32] Pattern-Oriented Software Forensics: A Foundation of Memory Forensics and Forensics of Things (ISBN: 978-1908043696)

[33] Software Narratology: An Introduction to the Applied Science of Software Stories (ISBN: 978-1908043078)

[34] Software Diagnostics Institute: www.TraceAnalysis.org

cyberspace narratives such as social media narratives (Facebook, Twitter[35], and LinkedIn) and even traditional media narratives such as news, stories, and books. Such pattern-oriented analysis of malnarratives can be used not only in security but also in intelligence analysis[36] and information operations (IO), for example, in information warfare (IW).

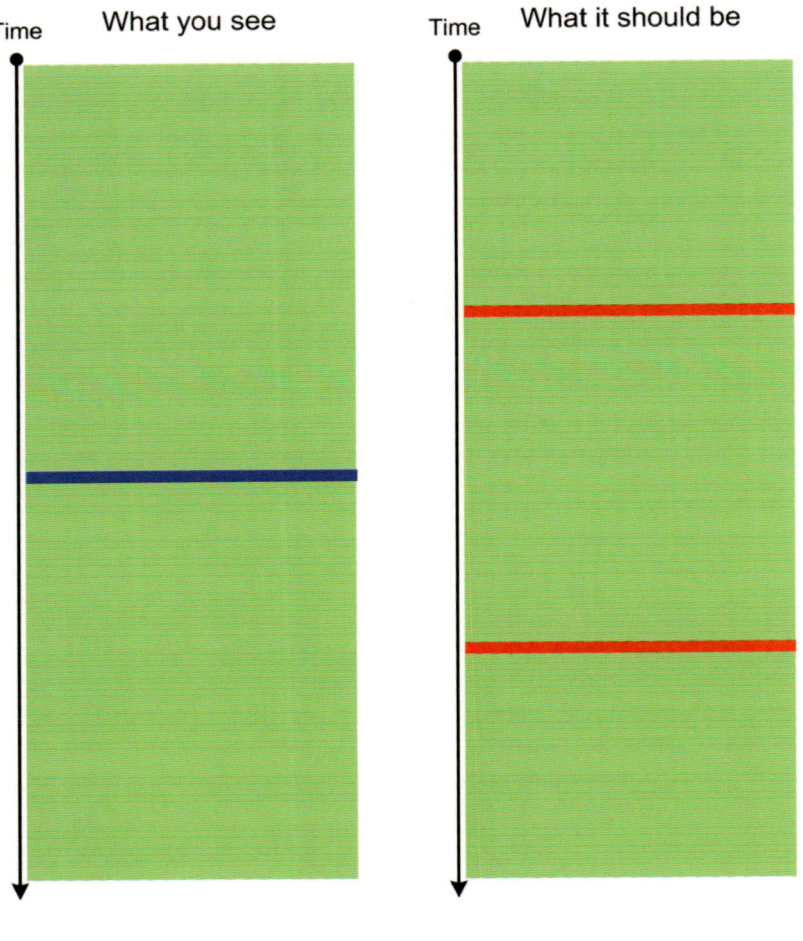

---

[35] The Structure of Twitter Narrative: Applied Patterns from Software Narratology and Human-Computer Narratives (ISBN: 978-1908043610)

[36] Memory Dump Analysis Anthology, Volume 6 (ISBN: 978-1908043191) p. 289.

Higher-Order Pattern Narratives (Analyzing Diagnostic Analysis)

A pattern narrative in software narratology means a narrative where messages or log entries are patterns from pattern catalogs. These can be either domain specific patterns or general trace and log analysis patterns such as **Discontinuity** (Volume 4, page 341), **Activity Region** (Volume 4, page 348), **Significant Event** (Volume 5, page 281), **Macrofunction** (Volume 7, page 283), and **Back Trace** (page 95). Generally, the software pattern narrative is a narrative constructed from software execution artifacts such as logs and memory dumps during their analysis. It is different from the usual meaning of a pattern narrative in narratology and literary criticism where we have a narrative that is a pattern itself like **Master Trace** (Volume 6, page 247) analysis pattern. So in our case it is a narrative of patterns and not a narrative that is a pattern. The following picture illustrates the correspondence between a software trace example and its software pattern narrative:

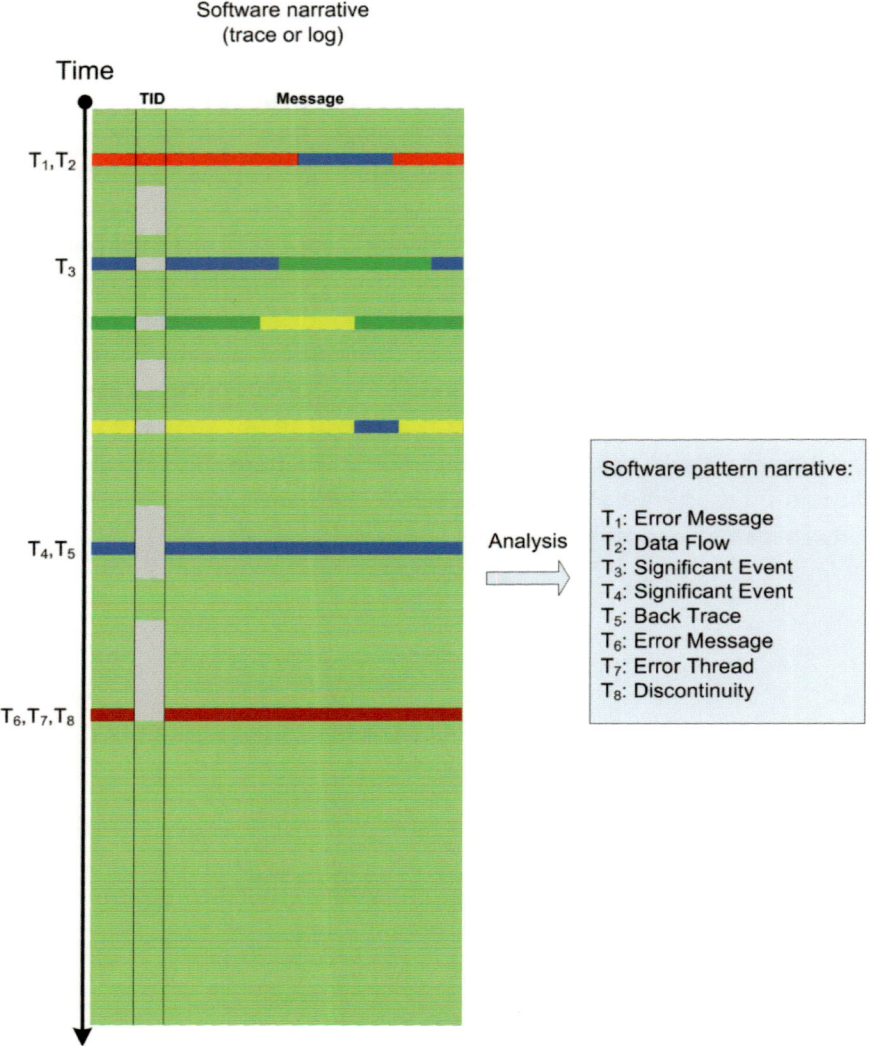

Software narrative
(trace or log)

A pattern narrative can be further analyzed for any missing patterns using pattern sequences and schemes.

By a second-order narrative, we mean a narrative about narrative such as the analysis of the original narrative (a first-order narrative). For example, the transformation of a software log into its pattern narrative equivalent (the so-called analysis narrative) is a second order narrative. It has its own time sequence (called Analysis Time, TA) where certain patterns are diagnosed out-of-order of their appearance in the resulting pattern narrative. In such a narrative, additional patterns may be included that were diagnosed initially but were later replaced or eliminated. The latter property shows that second-order narratives are not simply rearranged plots of the same story (fabula). In the case of generalized memory narratives and hybrid artifacts such as memory dumps, we also have analysis narratives. The following picture shows the analysis narrative used to construct a software pattern narrative from the previous picture example. We see what patterns were found first:

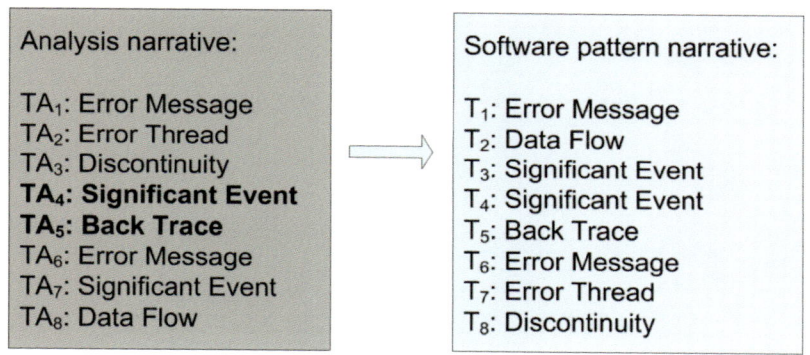

Such second-order narratives can be analyzed further and give rise to third-order narratives and in general to higher-order narratives. The following diagram shows the relationship between a software narrative (order N), its pattern narrative (order N) and analysis narrative (order N+1):

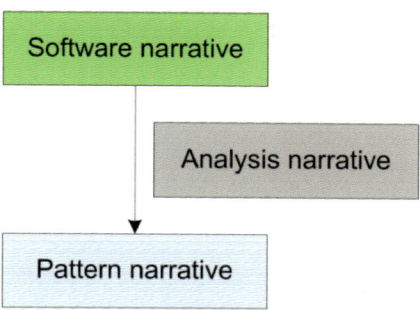

The same principles of software narratology and its analysis patterns can be applied here. **Discontinuities, Time Deltas,** and other patterns can be analyzed to find out analysis difficulties that might require further training (such as in domain-specific knowledge) and analysis tool development for subsequent computer assistance. For example, if we compare TAs in the analysis report above we find out that there was significant **Time Delta** pattern before **Back Trace** pattern was found leading to the first `Error Message` (Volume 7, page 299) pattern from a different `Thread of Activity` (Volume 4, page 339). It took some time for an analyst to get an idea to look for specific `Data Flow` (Volume 7, page 296) pattern and construct **Back Trace** (probably by looking at the source code).

If you are new to Software Narratology, please find this introduction:

http://www.patterndiagnostics.com/Introduction-Software-Narratology-materials

PART 8: Software Diagnostics, Troubleshooting, and Debugging

A Pattern Language for Performance Analysis

We introduce a new software diagnostics pattern sub-catalogue based on trace and log analysis patterns. It now includes the following performance analysis patterns (with more patterns added soon):

- **Counter Value** (Volume 7, page 288)
- Global Monotonicity
- Constant Value

Many general log analysis patterns based on software narratology are applicable to performance monitoring logs because they structure analysis data and corresponding thought process:

- **Adjoint Thread** (Volume 5, page 283, can be visualized via different colors on a graph)
- **Focus of Tracing** (Volume 6, page 243)
- **Characteristic Message Block** (Volume 4, page 345, for graphs)
- **Activity Region** (Volume 4, page 348)
- **Significant Event** (Volume 5, page 281) and many others

The goal is to discern, describe, and classify general regularities and their interactions in captured performance data including analysis approaches reused across different operating systems, products, and their performance monitoring and analysis tools. Such **Pattern-Oriented Performance Analysis** as a part of Pattern-Oriented Software Diagnostics includes pattern-driven, pattern-based, and systemic parts.

The Timeless Way of Diagnostics

Paraphrasing two classical books on architecture written by Christopher Alexander, et al. *"The Timeless Way of Building"* and *"A Pattern Language: Towns, Buildings, Construction"* we would like to introduce the complete restructuring of multivolume Memory Dump Analysis Anthology[37] into the projected ten-volume **"A Pattern Language for Software Diagnostics, Forensics, and Prognostics: Memory, Traces, Deconstruction"**. We plan the first volume for the beginning of 2015 (ISBN: 978-1908043818) and then releasing additional volume bi-monthly. The reference has better browsing and cross-referencing format, additional examples, and case studies. It incorporates comments and new pattern knowledge acquired since we described the first patterns 8 years ago. The new edition covers only patterns and does not include additional content found in Memory Dump Analysis Anthology such as philosophy and art. Here's the preliminary front cover based on Software Diagnostics Institute logo:

---

[37] http://www.dumpanalysis.org/advanced-software-debugging-reference

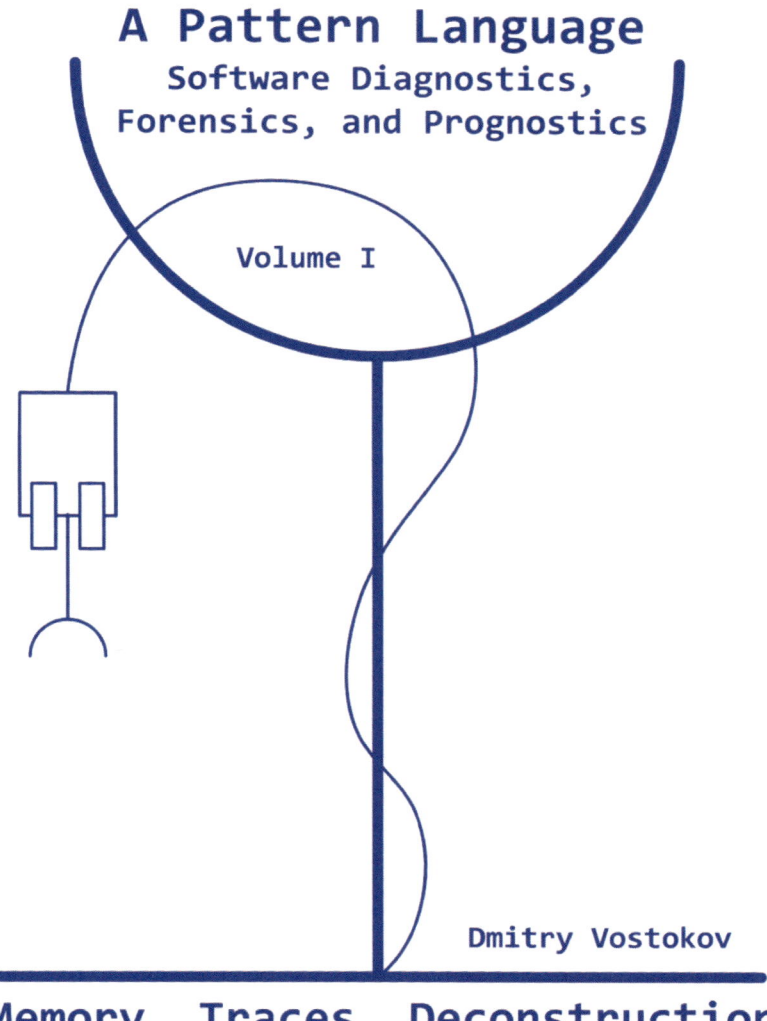

A Pattern Language

Software Diagnostics,
Forensics, and Prognostics

Volume I

Dmitry Vostokov

Memory, Traces, Deconstruction

Memory Dump Analysis Anthology continues to be released with Volume 8b planned for 2015. It includes up to date research from Software Diagnostics Institute and additional topics not included in "A Pattern Language for Software Diagnostics, Forensics, and Prognostics".

Pattern-Oriented Debugging Process

Modern debugging is complex and usually distributed across organizations involving many persons and teams:

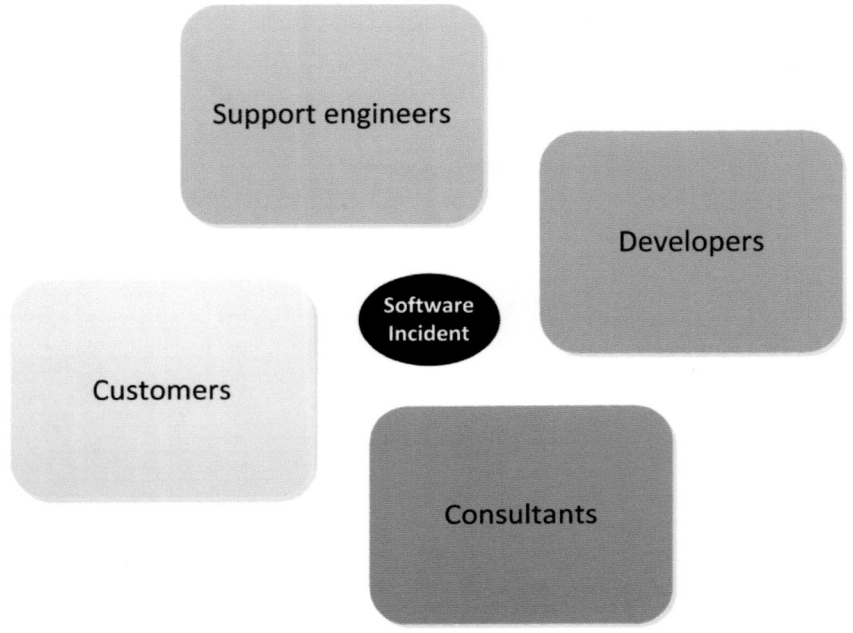

We propose a fully pattern-oriented debugging process that takes into account the integral role of software diagnostics and software construction patterns.

Whenever we have a software incident, we usually start with a small number of **Elementary Software Diagnostics Patterns**[38] to identify what kind of software execution artifacts to collect. Such artifacts may include memory dumps and logs for postmortem debugging but can also be running software itself, the so-called live debugging scenario. These patterns can be also called **Software Diagnostics Analysis Patterns** reflecting the fact that we need to analyze what we further need to do before doing software diagnostics itself.

---

[38] http://www.dumpanalysis.org/elementary-diagnostics-patterns

Based on artifacts we identify patterns of software behavior such as memory and trace analysis patterns. We call these patterns **Software Diagnostics Usage Patterns**.

Such usage patterns can be also called **Debugging Analysis Patterns** because we need to diagnose the right problem before doing any debugging.

Specific techniques reused across different software diagnostics and debugging scenarios we name **Software Diagnostics** and **Debugging Implementation Patterns**. There can also be **Debugging Usage Patterns** as reusable debugging scenarios.

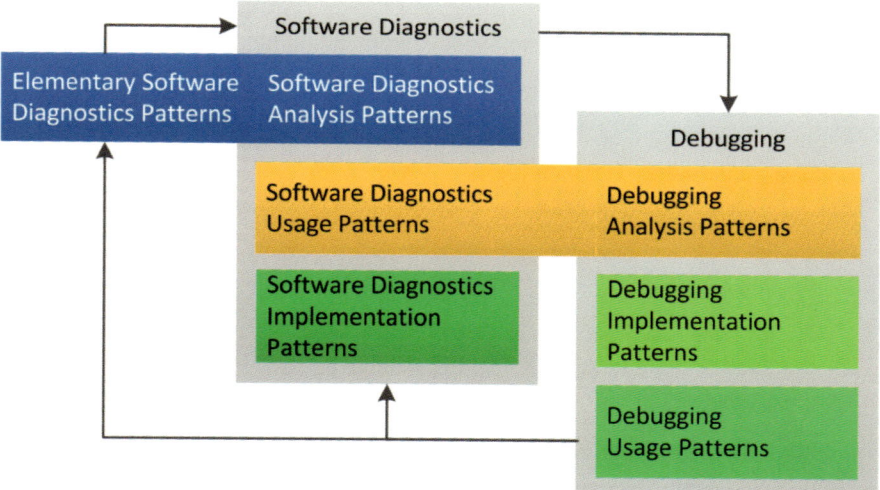

Previously we introduced Unified Debugging Patterns [39] (Analysis, Architecture, Design, Implementation, and Usage) to which we would like to add **Debugging Presentation Patterns** and similar *pattern stack* for software diagnostics:

---

[39] http://www.patterndiagnostics.com/PDSPSI-materials

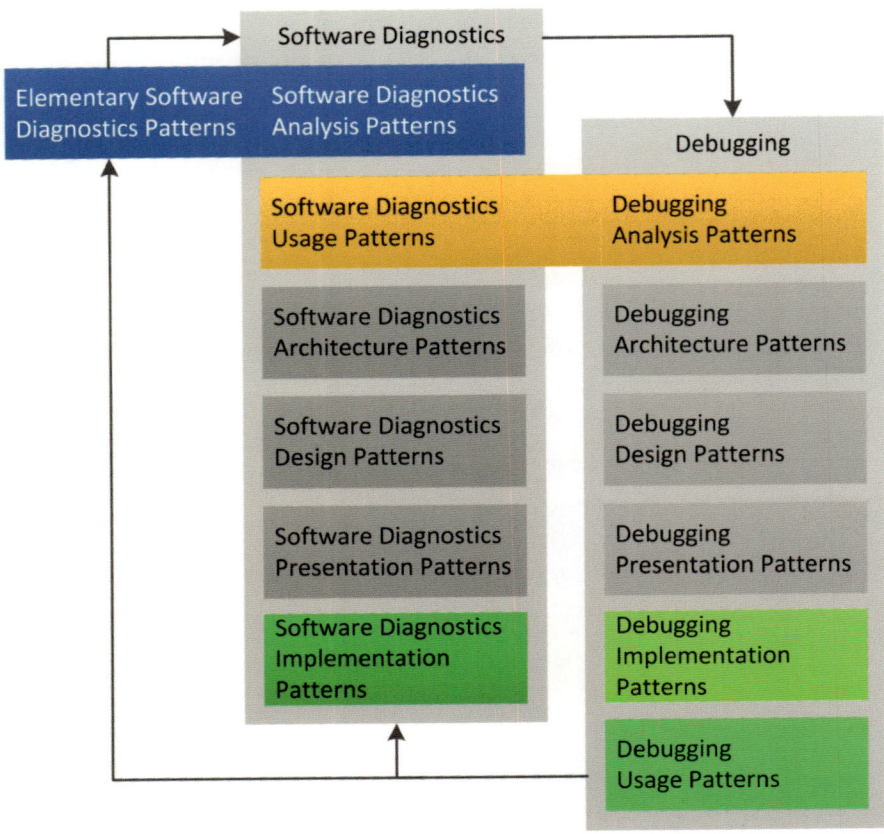

These pattern categories are usually already in existence and are important only when we develop new software diagnostics and debugging infrastructures and tools. For example, Patterns-View-Controller architectural pattern[40].

Examples of Elementary Software Diagnostics (Software Diagnostics Analysis) Patterns, Software Diagnostics Usage (Debugging Analysis) Patterns, and Debugging Implementation Patterns can be found in Accelerated Windows Debugging book[41].

---

[40] http://www.dumpanalysis.org/patterns-view-controller

[41] http://www.dumpanalysis.org/accelerated-windows-debugging-book

Café WoW

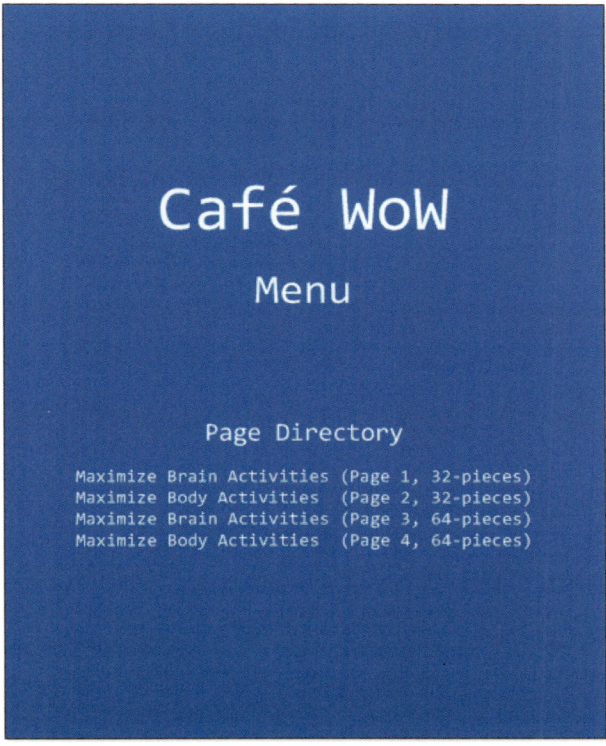

Bang Debugging

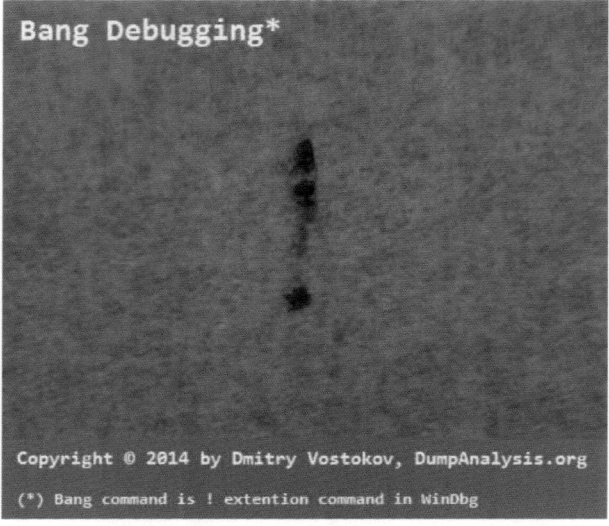

Bug Hunter

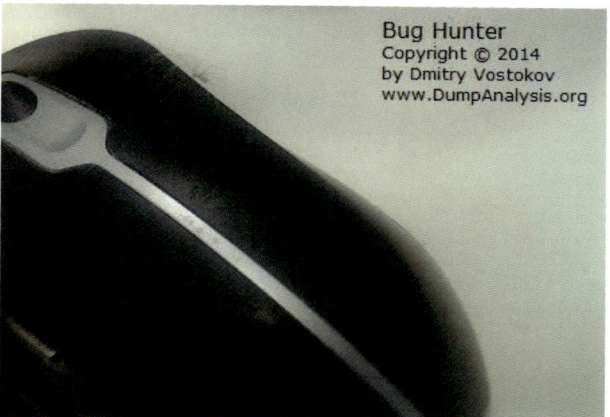

Glass of Water Dump

While a pessimist
developer discussed
a not fully filled
glass of water with
an optimist salesperson
a practical tester
smashed it into an
execution artefact.

Memory Dump Analysis

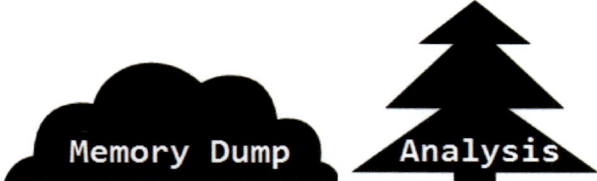

Organic Incidents and Bad Stench

- Organic Incidents

$$C_nH_m$$

n crashes, m hangs

- Bad Stench

$$H_2S$$

2 hangs, a spike

PART 10: Miscellaneous

Book Discovery

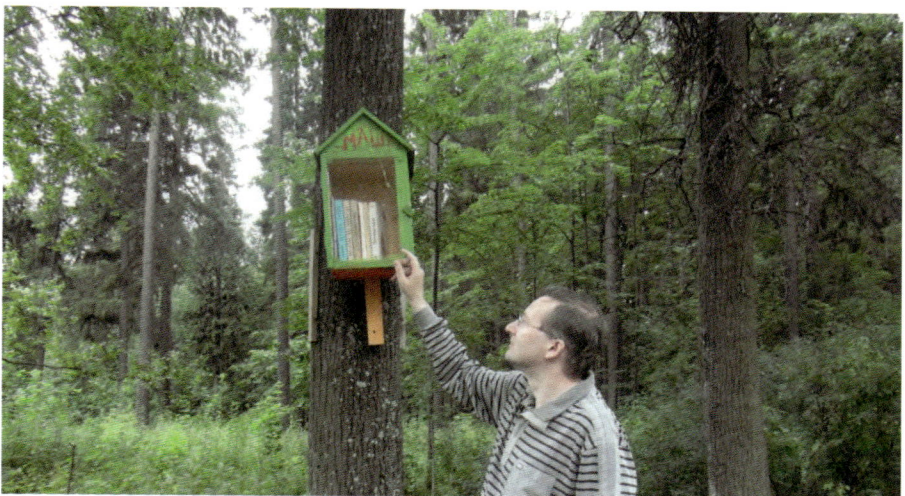

Quotes

These are my selected thoughts I posted previously on Facebook, Twitter, and where appropriate, on LinkedIn.

-   Fiction is for Diagnostics. Science Fiction is for Prognostics.

-   History is an exception. History starts with diagnostics.

-   You cannot fit a gigabyte into one byte, but you can stream through it.

-   Modern software traces require engineers to activate their neural networks.

-   Crash dump analysis No. 18643. "See crash dump analysis No. 14120".

-   A desire to bomb comes from the suppression of certain instincts during childhood.

-   A too perfect program is most likely malware. (*After reading "The Discovered Country" by Ian MacLeod*).

-   If it rains for too long, it may be a simulation.

-   Again, the German language helps to understand the essence of software. Hang (in German) - tendency.

-   After an hour of code come many hours of analysis.

-   A software support practitioner is a diplomat who brings peace to both sides: a user and a developer.

-   Win-Dbg is a situation you frequently discover when working with Windows. Neither Win-Win nor Win-Lose.

-   If I were a Unixoid, I would have moved to Windows because of WinDbg (WinningDbg).

- A dump analysis job is in some way similar to an accountant job - examining records of some company.

- "Terminal error" has two meanings: soft and hard.

- When you write defect-laden code, you need to follow coding standards otherwise you end up with defects inside defects and start debugging to make your defects correct. (*From the forthcoming "Software Defect Construction: Simulation and Modeling of Software Bugs"*).

- You only discover new patterns when you work slowly.

- I am a diagnostician. I only see problems. You have a problem. Your computer system is healthy.

- Intuition: pattern recall from internalized pattern catalogs. Therefore, pattern-oriented software diagnostics help increase your problem-solving intuition by diagnosing the right problem.

- Inaccessible Data Analysis is the next big thing.

- A good trace is one that has an answer when you search for "reason".

[This page is intentionally left blank]

Appendix

Crash Dump Analysis Checklist

General:

- Symbol servers (*.symfix*)
- Internal database(s) search
- Google or Microsoft search for suspected components as this could be a known issue. Sometimes a simple search immediately points to the fix on a vendor's site
- The tool used to save a dump (to flag false positive, incomplete or inconsistent dumps)
- OS/SP version (*version*)
- Language
- Debug time
- System uptime
- Computer name (*dS srv!srvcomputername* or *!envvar COMPUTERNAME*)
- List of loaded and unloaded modules (*lmv* or *!dlls*)
- Hardware configuration (*!sysinfo*)
- *.kframes 1000*

Application or service:

- Default analysis (*!analyze -v* or *!analyze -v -hang* for hangs)
- Critical sections (*!cs -s -l -o*, *!locks*) for both crashes and hangs
- Component timestamps, duplication and paths. DLL Hell? (*lmv* and *!dlls*)
- Do any newer components exist?
- Process threads (*~*kv* or *!uniqstack*) for multiple exceptions and blocking functions
- Process uptime
- Your components on the full raw stack of the problem thread
- Your components on the full raw stack of the main application thread
- Process size
- Number of threads
- Gflags value (*!gflag*)
- Time consumed by threads (*!runaway*)
- Environment (*!peb*)
- Import table (*!dh*)

- Hooked functions (*!chkimg*)
- Exception handlers (*!exchain*)
- Computer name (*!envvar COMPUTERNAME*)
- Process heap stats and validation (*!heap -s, !heap -s -v*)
- CLR threads? (*mscorwks* or *clr* modules on stack traces) Yes: use .NET checklist below
- Hidden (unhandled and handled) exceptions on thread raw stacks

System hang:

- Default analysis (*!analyze -v -hang*)
- ERESOURCE contention (*!locks*)
- Processes and virtual memory including session space (*!vm 4*)
- Important services are present and not hanging (for example, terminal or IMA services for Citrix environments)
- Pools (*!poolused*)
- Waiting threads (*!stacks*)
- Critical system queues (*!exqueue f*)
- I/O (*!irpfind*)
- The list of all thread stack traces (*!process 0 3f*)
- LPC/ALPC chain for suspected threads (*!lpc message* or *!alpc /m* after search for "*Waiting for reply to LPC*" or "*Waiting for reply to ALPC*" in *!process 0 3f* output)
- Mutants (search for "*Mutants - owning thread*" in *!process 0 3f* output)
- Critical sections for suspected processes (*!cs -l -o -s*)
- Sessions, session processes (*!session, !sprocess*)
- Processes (size, handle table size) (*!process 0 0*)
- Running threads (*!running*)
- Ready threads (*!ready*)
- DPC queues (*!dpcs*)
- The list of APCs (*!apc*)
- Internal queued spinlocks (*!qlocks*)
- Computer name (*dS srv!srvcomputername*)
- File cache, VACB (*!filecache*)
- File objects for blocked thread IRPs (*!irp -> !fileobj*)
- Network (*!ndiskd.miniports* and *!ndiskd.pktpools*)
- Disk (*!scsikd.classext -> !scsikd.classext class_device 2*)
- Modules rdbss, mrxdav, mup, mrxsmb in stack traces

BSOD:

- Default analysis (*!analyze -v*)
- Pool address (*!pool*)
- Component timestamps (*lmv*)
- Processes and virtual memory (*!vm 4*)
- Current threads on other processors
- Raw stack
- Bugcheck description (including ln exception address for corrupt or truncated dumps)
- Bugcheck callback data (*!bugdump* for systems prior to Windows XP SP1)
- Bugcheck secondary callback data (*.enumtag*)
- Computer name (*dS srv!srvcomputername*)
- Hardware configuration (*!sysinfo*)

.NET application or service:

- CLR module and SOS extension versions (*lmv* and *.chain*)
- Managed exceptions (*~*e !pe*)
- Nested managed exceptions (*!pe -nested*)
- Managed threads (*!Threads -special*)
- Managed stack traces (*~*e !CLRStack*)
- Managed execution residue (*~*e !DumpStackObjects* and *!DumpRuntimeTypes*)
- Managed heap (*!VerifyHeap, !DumpHeap -stat* and *!eeheap -gc*)
- GC handles (*!GCHandles, !GCHandleLeaks*)
- Finalizer queue (*!FinalizeQueue*)
- Sync blocks (*!syncblk*)

[This page is intentionally left blank]

Index of WinDbg Commands

!address, 52, 58, 63, 64, 65, 66, 67, 68, 79
!alpc, 15, 144
!analyze, 143, 144, 145
!bugdump, 145
!chkimg, 144
!CLRStack, 73, 75, 76, 145
!cs, 78, 143, 144
!dh, 143
!dlls, 143
!do, 74, 76
!dpcs, 144
!dso, 73, 75
!DumpHeap, 145
!DumpRuntimeTypes, 145
!DumpStackObjects, 145
!eeheap, 145
!envvar, 143, 144
!exchain, 144
!exqueue, 144
!filecache, 144
!fileobj, 144
!FinalizeQueue, 145
!fltkd, 49
!GCHandleLeaks, 145
!GCHandles, 145
!gflag, 52, 74, 143
!handle, 33
!heap, 57, 59, 63, 64, 144
!irp, 16, 46, 49, 144
!irpfind, 16, 144
!locks, 143, 144
!lpc, 144
!ndiskd.miniports, 144
!ndiskd.pktpools, 144
!pe, 70, 75, 145
!peb, 143
!pool, 145
!poolused, 144
!process, 144

!qlocks, 144
!ready, 144
!runaway, 60, 143
!running, 144
!scsikd.classext, 144
!session, 144
!sprocess, 144
!stacks, 144
!syncblk, 145
!sysinfo, 143, 145
!teb, 39
!thread, 16, 33, 46, 78
!Threads, 145
!uniqstack, 143
!VerifyHeap, 145
!vm, 144, 145
!process, 144
.chain, 145
.cxr, 18, 21, 28, 31
.ecxr, 18
.enumtag, 145
.for, 13
.frame, 31, 32, 72
.kframes, 143
.load, 70
.process, 77
.symfix, 143
.thread, 18, 28, 30, 31, 78
~, 143, 145
~*kv, 143
dp, 32
dps, 21, 52, 61
dpS, 39
dS, 143, 144, 145
dt, 31
k, 17, 18, 21, 28, 43, 51, 71, 74
kc, 60, 81
kn, 31, 72
lmv, 70, 143, 145
ln, 145

s, 143, 144
ub, 51, 73

uf, 30